Strategic Sourcing

Suppliers are from Mars
Customers are from Venus

2nd Edition

Murillo Cesar Xavier

Xavier, Murillo C. *Strategic Sourcing - Suppliers are from Mars, Customers are from Venus*. 2nd ed. Lulu, 2010.

Copyright© 2010
All rights reserved.
POD at Lulu.com

ISBN: 978-0-557-31172-9

Index:

Foreword 3

Preface 5

Section I –Strategic Sourcing Evolution 7

1. Signs of Evolution 9

   1.1 – A Brief History of Business Integration 12

   1.2 – Embracing Evolution 14

   1.3 – Lessons from Venus and Mars 19

2. What is Strategic Sourcing? 20

3. Best Practices 28

   3.1 - Leadership is Essential 29

   3.2 - Total Cost Rather Than Price 30

   3.3 - Strategic Sourcing is Fact Based 33

   3.4 - Technology is your Friend 34

   3.5 - Be a Strategic Thinker 35

   3.6 – Communication is Key 36

Section II –Implementation Process 39

4. Strategic Sourcing Road Map 41

5. Business Case 49

   5.1 – Internal Analysis 51

   5.2 – External Analysis 54

   5.3 – Opportunities 57

      5.3.1 – Cost of Goods 57

      5.3.2 – Business Processes 58

      5.3.3 – Sourcing Strategies 59

   5.4 – Business Case Presentation 61

6. Profiling 63

   6.1 – Sourcing Tree 64

   6.2 – The Sourcing Implementation Matrix 66

7. Alternative Creation 70
7.1 – Partnerships 74
  7.1.1 – Vertical Integration 74
  7.1.2 – Strategic Alliances 77
7.2 – Rationalization 80
7.3 – Negotiation 83
7.4 – Organizational Structure 84

8. Alternative Selection 87
8.1 – Strategy Selection 88
8.2 – Supplier Selection 89

9. Delivery 94
9.1 – Operational Integration 94
9.2 – Hand-off 99
9.3 – Follow up 100

10. Change Management 102

Section III – Case Studies 109

11. Mini-case I: Freight Analysis 111
11.1 – Rationalization 112
11.2 – Strategy 114
11.3 – Negotiation 116
11.4 – Organizational Structure 117
11.5 – Conclusion 118

12. Mini-case II: Capital Investment 120

13. Mini-case III: Raw Material 128
13.1 – Rationalization 129
13.2 – Strategy 137
13.3 – Negotiation 138
13.4 – Organizational Structure 138
13.5 – Conclusion 139

14. Frequently asked questions 140

Bibliography 150

Foreword

Focusing purely on growing their revenue is no longer enough for corporations to stay ahead of the competition. With an ever-increasing number of players in the battlefield, organizations have been forced to look for creative ways to be more competitive. This is the main reason why Strategic Sourcing has become a fundamental philosophy in reinventing the way business is done.

Companies that fully embraced the concept and successfully implemented strategic sourcing as a way to differentiate them have been able to strategically manage spending and develop a competitive advantage.

Although many companies recognize the importance of developing a Strategic Sourcing capability, many fail to implement a successful corporate-wide program and effectively generate and maximize all the benefits of such a program.

Companies usually focus primarily on external factors and underestimate the importance of internal aspects. Organizations typically drive their initiatives by spending most of their efforts and resources on supplier selection and pricing negotiations (external issues), yet overlook key internal factors, such as organizational change, decision making processes, and relationship building.

Whether addressing internal or external challenges, relationship building is critical to strategically drive sourcing initiatives and capitalize on its benefits. From an external perspective, building solid relationships with strategic suppliers is fundamental to assuring supply continuity, achievement of business needs, improvement in quality standards, and acquisition of market intelligence. On the other hand, building relationships with internal business partners is essential to securing stakeholder buy-in, assure high compliance levels, and generate sustainable savings.

Suppliers are from Mars, Customers are from Venus provides a comprehensive description of what Strategic Sourcing is all about. Murillo Xavier also describes the major challenges corporations have been facing when building such a capability, and discusses best practices to overcome them.

It is well known that Strategic Sourcing can become a powerful competitive advantage and help companies to stay ahead of the competition. The challenge lies on how to successfully implement a program that effectively delivers sustainable results. By using case studies illustrating a detailed road map, the author explains how to build a strategic sourcing competence in any organization.

Additionally, Murillo Xavier describes the implementation process in a very creative and easy-to-read way. Having relationship building as the stepping-stone, the author emphasizes the importance of partnerships to productively drive sourcing initiatives more strategically. Particularly, the author traces a parallel between business and personal relationships, making understanding of the topic very accessible to anyone, with or without experience on this field.

Whether you want to build an effective Strategic Sourcing philosophy in your organization, or simply improve your overall understanding of this subject, this book is definitely a great source of knowledge.

Elvin Zung
Strategic Sourcing Manager
GAP Inc.

Preface

"When men and women are able to respect and accept their differences then love has a chance to blossom."

John Gray, PhD

When Dr. John Gray wrote *Men are from Mars, Women are from Venus*, he disseminated the idea that men and women have fundamental differences in their ways of thinking, acting, and interpreting the world around them.

Many of the conflicts in relationships come from poor understanding of partners. For example, not knowing what your partner wants, or how to communicate your own expectations may damage your chances to explore the full potential of the relationship.

It is astonishing how some leaders were successful in growing healthy personal relationships, but were unable to do the same in business. Maybe they have not realized that some basic principles apply in both cases. Perhaps, they have not realized that Suppliers are from Mars, and Customers are from Venus too. They also speak different languages, and have some fundamental differences that hinder the progress of the companies.

Lack of trust, an adversarial mindset, inefficient communication, and poor affinity are just some of the challenges that restrict them from unlocking all the potential of their business partnerships.

That is when the importance of Strategic Sourcing becomes evident. More than a tool or technique, Strategic Sourcing is a philosophy that helps companies to identify business partners, and explore all the benefits of the relationship.

In the first section of the book, we introduce Strategic Sourcing, demonstrating its importance in today's competitive world, and giving a few tips on the best practices for its implementation.

The second section brings a more academic view of the implementation process of a traditional Strategic Sourcing project.

Finally, the third part shows three mini-cases selected to highlight some specific points of the implementation process. Although these cases were based on real companies, all the names and sensitive data were changed to preserve their identities.

Strategic Sourcing is a vast subject, and no publication can capture all the nuances contained in different projects and techniques. The sourcing strategies a company can use will depend on many factors, such as the product being acquired, market trends, and availability of partners, etc.

Consequently, this book does not have the pretension of exhausting the topic, but shows the basic steps and tools for the implementation of Strategic Sourcing. It will highlight some of the main impacts of this kind of project on organizations, and give a few examples of possible strategies a company may consider in order to succeed.

Section I
Strategic Sourcing Evolution

Chapter 1

Signs of Evolution

"In the long history of humankind (and animal kind, too) those who learned to collaborate and improvise most effectively have prevailed."

Charles Darwin

I have always thought fairy tales were created not to make children sleep, but to make grown-ups awake. In each story, there is a message to open our eyes for something hidden in our minds. Every time I read or tell one of these stories, I learn a little more.

A few months ago, I was telling my 6-year-old niece the Little Red Riding Hood story. I told her how brave the little girl was, going by herself to take some goodies to her old grandma. Suddenly, my niece interrupted me with innumerable questions:

- How did the Wolf stop her? Wasn't there a police officer around? Why did she talk to a stranger? Why didn't she call her parents on the cell phone? Didn't she have a cell phone?!?!?

The next day, I decided to try the Snow White story. After telling my little niece about the Magic Mirror on the wall that knew everything, she asked me if that was a kind of Internet.

What next? I thought I could try the Hansel & Gretel story where the two kids get lost in the woods and find a gingerbread house. However, I was afraid my little niece would ask me if the kids had a GPS, or about the impact of gingerbread on a low-carb diet!

I was a little frustrated. Kids are growing up faster and smarter than they used to. They are growing in a new world with new standards, behavior, and technology. It took 38 years for the radio to reach 50 million users. It took 16 years for PCs to reach the same number of users For TVs it took

13 years and for the Internet only 4 years. That shows how fast our world is assimilating new technologies.

But don't let stories about a 6-year-old girl convince you of the importance of being aware of the latest technologies and trends. Just look around and draw your own conclusions.

The competitive business environment has reduced the profit margins for virtually all segments along the years. Companies, which used to have a margin of fifty per cent for some products, now have less than five.

In order to improve their financial health, some companies created very aggressive cost reduction programs. At some point, these programs reach the boundaries of the companies, and the executives realized that, in order to reduce their costs, they would have to work with their external partners.

To improve procurement activities, the executives knew they should not focus only on price. They would have to transform the way they were doing business, not only within their companies, but also in their relationship with their business partners.

For many years, consulting companies have conducted complex projects to improve sourcing initiatives for their clients. However, it was only in the 90's that we could observe a real mobilization of the companies toward sourcing strategies.

Companies have started paying more attention in the supply function and have created new departments in order to coordinate and improve their actions. Internal processes and purchase decisions were aligned to customer needs, vendor capabilities, financial constraints, life cycle costs, the overall company strategy, and many other factors.

In the last few years, several factors have expanded the offer of vendors and products. New technologies have made it easy to search globally for companies able to attend to our requirements. New economic blocks have also contributed to the availability of products and services around the world. Therefore, executives in every company had to re-evaluate their entire supply network. They had to consider the new possibilities available in the market, and start pursuing new opportunities.

Some companies have already realized the potential of Strategic Sourcing. They saw that purchases of goods and services could consume as much as 70% or more of a business' revenues. In light of that, they started playing an aggressive game.

Not long ago, Michael D. Eisner, the CEO of The Walt Disney Company announced they were targeting annual savings of $300 million using Strategic Sourcing initiatives. Disney established the Strategic Sourcing and Procurement organization connecting the central corporate and all of Disney's businesses. The organization pursues efficiencies in different parts of the Disney group: analyzing sourcing, procurement, inventory management, warehousing, transportation and logistics, customer fulfillment, and call-center management.

DuPont set itself the goal of reducing fixed costs by $700 million, with more than half of that coming from savings in contract services, supplies procurement, telecommunications, and information technology.

IBM was committed to deliver a 5% sustained competitive advantage, net of price variations across its entire portfolio of external purchases.

Top executives at BellSouth asked the company's sourcing department to bank $1billion or more worth of savings in three years. The group delivered $1.1 billion in the first year.

The State of California has achieved a 38% average cost reduction over their telecommunication contracts, and expects to save over $20 million in two years with their new Strategic Sourcing initiative.

Those responsible for these organizations have already realized the potential of Strategic Sourcing. In many cases, a simple 10% reduction in outside purchasing cost can increase the profitability of the company from 20% to 60%. In fact, some companies re-evaluated their suppliers and achieved savings of more than 40% by using regional suppliers instead of national ones.

With Strategic Sourcing, many companies, financial institutions, governmental offices, and other organizations are achieving double-digit-percentage cost savings, and are improving their relationship with suppliers, causing a positive impact on the quality of their products and services.

There are many benefits companies experience when they implement Strategic Sourcing. Cost reduction is just one of them. Other competitive advantages usually experienced are: standardization of processes, reduction of cycle times, greater use of cross-functional teams, gain of suppliers and market intelligence, quality improvements, access to leading edge technology, improvement of delivery times, and availability when supply is scarce.

All these magnificent results would not be possible without strong relationships. We are not only talking about external partners, but also an internal integration of departments and processes in order to dramatically improve results.

By now, you probably have already realized that if you own or manage a business, you should not ignore Strategic Sourcing. It does not matter whether you are in an executive position or not. Strategic Sourcing is a growing trend in all organizational levels, segments, and businesses.

Many big players have already started in this game. Consequently, the survival of many companies in the future may depend on how fast they can adopt a Strategic Sourcing program.

1.1 – A Brief History of Business Integration

It is interesting how relationships have evolved in the last few decades. Many social changes have transformed the dynamics of relationships. Equality movements, changes in the divorce and harassment laws, and new ways of communication are just a few examples of factors that have affected the modern relationships.

Therefore, in order to understand how Strategic Sourcing has evolved, let's step back into the past and have a quick look into the history of business integration.

In 1911, Frederick Taylor published his work about the principles of Scientific Management. Taylor showed the world how to improve the performance of the individual by analyzing and defining the best way a task could be performed. A few years later, Henry Ford opened the first moving assembly line using Taylor's theories and starting the modern model of mass production.

Reacting to Taylor theories, which, from a very simplistic point of view, considered men as a piece of equipment, Elton Mayo developed studies analyzing the work environment based on Human Relations. This new school of thought evolved into theories promoting the internal integration of areas, workers, and processes using tools, such as job rotation. These theories would take advantage of possible synergies not explored by Taylor's model. The basic idea was that the employee could perform better by understanding the needs of his direct customers.

However, it was only after the World War II that we could observe a real step towards supplier integration with Taiichi Ohno developing the Toyota Production System. One of the key components of this system was the concept of Just-in-Time, which required close collaboration from the vendors.

The technological advance experienced throughout the 80's and 90's allowed companies to achieve greater levels of integration with suppliers. However, many of these developments were still focusing on isolated actions instead of a coordinated strategy.

Some scholars believe that after reaching Supply Chain Integration, the next step of the evolution will be Industry Integration, then Cross-Industry Integration.

Although the rules for the next evolutionary steps are not clear, scholars believe that in the Industry Integration stage, companies would team up with their competitors, sharing not only basic functions, but also production plans, capacity information, and sales demand. However, this information would not flow freely among the companies. They would be shared in a way in which it would still be possible to preserve a competitive environment.

For instance, all the sensitive information could be shared only with a third party organization, which would assure confidentiality and avoid the competitors having access to each other data. By having access to the data of the whole industry, this central organization would be able to analyze all the inputs and provide guidance to the entire industry in order to minimize logistics costs, and to avoid things like overproduction and excessive inventories.

This scenario does sound like a utopia, though some consulting companies and industry organizations are already talking about offering this kind of services on a smaller scale.

The idea of Cross-Industry Integration comes from the fact that companies in different industries may have common interests. Therefore, organizations may look for integration opportunities outside their own environment, exchanging information and coordinating actions towards similar interests in order to achieve operational savings.

Achieving Cross-Industry Integration can be very challenging. A different industry may bring new paradigms. In other words, it may be a new way to communicate and interpret the facts. If suppliers are from Mars, and customers are from Venus, companies in different industries may be from Pluto.

As we can see, the business world has experienced great improvements due to integration. Strong relationships are the key to good integration. Therefore, knowing how to build and maintain partnerships is an essential skill for future business leaders.

1.2 – Embracing Evolution

In the 60's the Swiss were known for their powerful watch-making industry. They had 65% of the world market share and over 80% of the profits. A few years later, their market share declined to less than 10%, and many of those companies could not survive. This historical case is described in many business schools as an example of an industry that could not deal with changes. They closed their eyes to the evolution that was knocking on their doors.

The Swiss failed to understand that the evolution of the quartz watch would transform their business. Curiously, it was a Swiss who developed this new technology, starting the "Quartz Revolution." Regrettably, he could not convince his colleagues of the new opportunities his invention would bring. They were blinded by their old paradigm. The Swiss watchmakers could not accept that something with no bearings, gears, nor mainspring could be a thousand times more accurate than their prestigious watches.

The new invention was presented in the annual watch conference in 1967. Texas Instruments and Seiko saw the potential of the invention, and quickly assimilated the new technology. That event marked the decline of the Swiss watch-making industry.

Sometimes it is not easy to embrace the changes evolution brings. For personal relationships, there is always "the next step" people are hesitant to take. Commitments such as getting married, living together, or having kids, involve great transformations of behavior, lifestyle, responsibility, etc. People are usually afraid of changes because of the uncertainty they bring.

In the same way, changes in the business environment may bring adverse reactions from those involved in the transformation. People do not like to leave their comfort zone. They are used to certain processes, and habits.

It does not mean that changes are always good. However, some of them are unavoidable, and the sooner companies realize that, the greater their chances of survival are. The truth is that some companies just cannot make the necessary changes. If we compare the list of the Fortune 500 from 10 years ago to today's list, we will see that 50% of the companies are missing.

Evolution in the market may change the value proposition expected by the customers. In a very short time, the market may impose new qualification criteria, and the companies who whish to survive may have to change. Basically, there are two positions an organization can assume while dealing with this kind of market evolution. A company can be either an "Evolutionary Agent," or a "Target Species."

An Evolutionary Agent is a visionary who will define the new standard for products, services, or processes for the industry. Others observe the movements of this company and follow its steps. In other words, it will cause market evolution in order to assume a leading position and create strategic advantage.

Being an Evolutionary Agent may be risky since they hold the responsibility of walking unexplored paths. However, organizations with this profile are very flexible to changes and can adapt to the most diverse situations.

Steve Jobs is an example of an Evolutionary Agent. Every organization he leads, pro-actively seeks new technologies to set the standard for the rest of the industry. He is a visionary with a life marked by innovations, which his competitors try to copy. The founder of Apple has always emphasized the importance of design, developing products that are both functional and aesthetic. It is easy to see this trend in his work from the first Macintosh computer to the phenomenal success of the iPod.

Steve Jobs also integrated entertainment and technology, setting a new standard for the industry by creating Pixar, one of the most successful animation studios in the world.

Jobs' ability in building strong partnerships is key in the business evolution process. Steve Jobs is a master in relationships, and uses his experience and charisma to bring different partners together to materialize new ideas. He has the power of making people around him feel comfortable with changes. Steve Jobs makes changing and evolving look as natural as breathing.

Being a Target Species might sound less risky than being an Evolution Agent, since it does not require dedicating time and resources looking for breakthroughs. However, organizations that fail to realize the need for changes, or to create and execute a transformation plan, may perish like many of the Swiss watchmakers. Therefore, the Target Species face the risk of blindness or difficulty to catch up with the new market requirements.

Some of the Swiss watch manufacturers realized their survival would depend on their capacity of adapting to a new reality. Some manufacturers decided not to change their processes and maintain their old style. Instead of using quartz, they appealed to their experience and tradition, competing in quality and design positioning their products as luxury items. Rolex, for example, is one of these companies. Their quartz models never exceeded 7% of the company's total production.

Other well-known Swiss watch manufacturers such as Omega, Longines, Blancpain, Tissot, Rado, and Hamilton formed a consortium to avoid bankruptcy. This group achieved vertical integration, building a dense and dedicated network of suppliers. They re-created their manufacturing process, migrating from a handcraft to a mass production environment. Therefore, they were able to compete in price and quality to ensure their existence. Later, this consortium adopted the name of "The Swatch Group."

As we can see, managing changes is not an easy job. There is a lot of strategy and hard work involved. IBM is another good example of an organization that went under a revitalization process after realizing the market evolution.

Although IBM was one of the leaders in mainframes and systems, it was not well positioned to cope with the changes when the PC market became saturated in the late 80's. Consequently, IBM saw its profitability declining to an alarming level.

In 1993, Lou Gerstner was named IBM's new CEO. Instead of trying to do the same things better as his predecessor, John Akers, Gerstner had bold plans to do new things believing that a major change was the only way IBM could survive.

Advances in supply chain integration allowed IBM to achieve dramatic improvements. For example, the company centralized its purchasing and streamlined its production processes, which led to improvements in order fulfillment. Across the company, IBM consolidated old fragmented systems and, as one example of integration, went from 150 different accounting systems down to one.

Communication was an important factor for the transformation plan inside and outside the company. Understanding that he needed to court his customers, Lou Gerstner, soon after taking over, met personally with business partners and customers to explain the changes taking place in IBM. In addition, Gerstner introduced a new marketing campaign changing the culture and behavior of front line employees.

Another major component of IBM's transformation process was the focus on e-business. Some of the manifestations of IBM as an e-business leader involved e-commerce, e-procurement, e-care for business partners, e-care for customers, and e-care for influencers.

Through its new strategy, IBM started focusing on clients, new product development, technology tools, flexibility, and responsiveness. Distancing itself from its old rigid hierarchy, IBM started utilizing a matrix structure with decentralized decision-making. IBM got away from linear, product focused, highly reactive processes by integrating its planning, purchasing, and budgeting processes using the latest IT tools. The organization also introduced a new reward system based on performance, promoting integration and teamwork rather that recognizing only individual achievement.

In summary, Lou Gerstner realized the need for change and led a major transformation in processes, strategy, and corporate culture that brought IBM back to the forefront of the market.

Strategic Sourcing is an unavoidable market evolution. Re-thinking the relationship with partners and creating new supply strategies will not be a simple competitive advantage, but a requirement in the new business landscape. Remember that only the most adapted will survive. Therefore, do not ignore the evolution. Embrace it!

1.3 – Lessons from Venus and Mars

Strategic Sourcing is a growing trend in today's world. Since it is strongly based on business integration, executives have to have a more in-depth understanding of the dynamics of relationships. That is when Venus and Mars come to the rescue.

Business and personal relationships are not that different. They share the same basic concepts. Some executives would say that even the emotional component present in personal relationships can be found in the business world.

Some of the common points in the business and personal relationships involve:

- Finding the right partner;

- Establishing common long and short-term goals;

- Learning how to work together towards the same objectives;

- Growing and sharing experiences and expectations;

- Understanding the relationship and committing to its improvement; and

- Agreeing on the individual contributions and limitations of each partner.

In conclusion, Venus and Mars should be used as a reference in order to guide leaders in the creation of healthy business relationship, and to assure the success of any Strategic Sourcing initiative.

Chapter 2

What is Strategic Sourcing?

"Anyone who stops learning is old, whether at twenty or eighty. Anyone who keeps learning stays young. The greatest thing in life is to keep your mind young."

Henry Ford

In 1999, the company I was working for asked me to join a Supply Chain conference in South America to learn about the latest trends in the area. It may sound strange to many Supply Chain professionals, but one of the most interesting presentations in the conference was not given by a typical manufacturing company; it was given by a bank.

Mr. Zolla, the presenter, was the Director of Strategic Sourcing of the bank – an engineer who had worked for years in the IT and purchasing areas of great companies such as Shell, Alcoa, and Ford. For the last 3 years, he had been implementing a plan to achieve a 30% reduction in the total expenditures of the bank.

The hyperinflation and heavy taxes in most of South America forced the financial institutions in these countries accelerate their development in terms of processes and technology. Quality and efficiency were always top concerns for these organizations. Therefore, a 30% reduction in the expenditures could be viewed as a very challenging goal.

However, Mr. Zolla believed that a 30% reduction was a good target for a bank, but manufacturing companies could aspire to even better results, since the higher complexity of their supply chains could be hiding even more opportunities.

The executive of the bank shared with the audience his experience of creating a Strategic Sourcing area. When he started in the company, he analyzed the current situation and brought up a list of problems he had identified to the board of directors. Some of the main items were:

Chapter 2 – What is Strategic Sourcing? 📖 21

- Lack of Organization – the buyers did not have a strong process or tools in place to communicate with the vendors and with other areas of the bank.

- Internal Education – very few people in the organization knew the correct procedure to place a purchase request. Therefore, many orders could not be filled in the proper way.

- Payment Problems – there was a gap between purchases and accounts payable. Many vendors stop using the bank due to late payments.

- Market Intelligence – The buyer didn't know important characteristics about the products and the supplier's market.

- Obsolescence – Many inventories contained obsolete items.

- High Costs – The operational cost of the bank for maintenance, promotional materials, and other items was higher than the industry average.

- Number of Buyers - The number of buyers per employee was also considered above the industry average.

- Incorrect orders – There was an extremely high number of incorrect orders or late deliveries of the materials purchased.

- Suppliers – Many times the negotiation with suppliers were made on the spot. The bank counted with only a few regular suppliers, with no clear criteria by which to select them.

The executive highlighted to the board of directors that all those problems were obstructing the growth of the business. They were affecting the competitiveness of the bank, not only in a financial way, but also in the perception of its clients.

The clients were already feeling the inefficiencies of the bank. Some basic services could not be performed with the quality expected by them. For example, due to the problems in the purchasing process, ATM cards issued by the bank were taking weeks to get to the clients instead of days as in other banks.

Regarding these problems, Mr. Zolla drew an analogy between personal and business relationships: "Problems in the relationship of a couple can affect the entire family. In business, it is the same. Problems with our partners may affect the ones we love: the customers!" I believe that was the moment I started to see some similarities between personal and business relationships. Business, as life, is supported by a network of relationships. In order to succeed, one has to master the art of relationships. This is exactly one of the main points in Strategic Sourcing: improve and explore the relationships with the different partners. As Mr. Zolla was explaining, several factors contribute to that.

Mr. Zolla said that the Purchasing Department was the link between the company and the upstream partners (suppliers). He explained to the other executives of the bank that they had a Procurement Department but not a Purchasing Department. According to Mr. Zolla, the activities involving Purchasing should be split in two clear areas: Procurement and Sourcing.

In **Sourcing**, we have all the activities that give intelligence to the purchasing process. It is where the group studies the items to be bought, evaluates the market, works with the other areas in order to reduce the consumption, defines purchasing strategies, changes processes, and evaluates suppliers.

Procurement is the area responsible for the daily activities of coordinating requisitions, contracts, ordering, receiving, and managing the relationship with the suppliers.

A Strategic Sourcing company should have both of these areas (sourcing and procurement) well developed so that the Purchasing Department can create a strategy to align the internal processes and requirements to the trends and capabilities of the market. Figure 2-1 illustrates the difference between Procurement and Purchasing as explained by Mr. Zolla.

Mr. Zolla affirmed that fixing the processes could give them only marginal savings. His words were: "We had never had intelligence in this process. We had never studied what or why we were buying things. Fixing the current process without understanding the big picture won't give us an advantage over our competitors."

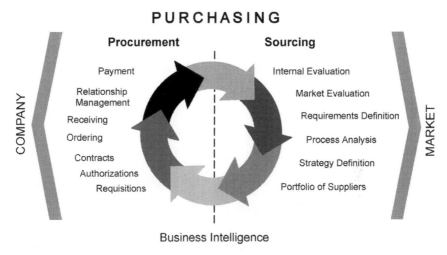

Figure 2-1: Purchasing Process - Procurement vs. Sourcing

The more someone knows about the partner, the better are the chances the relationship will work. This knowledge increases the chances of a good alignment in processes and goals. Knowing your partner is the number one rule for success in any kind of relationship.

Adding intelligence to a process sounds very logical. However, it is not very common to observe a structure in purchasing devoted to create this intelligence. This task usually falls to the purchasing analyst or manager, who has to couple this with his regular purchasing activities such as ordering, managing contract, and others. Consequently, we may observe problems in the integration between the Business and the Market. This is the missing link, key for great opportunities in any organization.

Therefore, Mr. Zolla proposed the creation of a Strategic Sourcing Area in the bank. This area would be responsible for understanding the organization and items being purchased. Furthermore, it would re-evaluate the entire process, and define new strategies for purchasing.

Based on the potential savings presented by Mr. Zolla, the bank executives authorized the creation of the new Strategic Sourcing Area and the implementation of the new philosophy.

By studying each material and bundling them into different categories, the new Strategic Sourcing Area defined a specific strategy for the procurement of each category. The strategy behind each material/service group was linked to the needs and overall strategy of the bank.

After 3 years, Mr. Zolla delivered the savings he promised. The bank had faster and more reliable purchasing tools, and customers could feel an improvement in the overall quality of the bank.

Since that presentation, I have been studying Strategic Sourcing and its implementation in many companies. It is impressive how fast an organization can change during such implementation.

In contrast to many quality programs, Strategic Sourcing does not target gradual improvements, but a complete reengineering of the supply organization. It enables buyers and suppliers to connect quickly and efficiently.

First, Strategic Sourcing will analyze all items purchased in order to define and implement new strategies and tools for their acquisition. Once that stage is completed, Strategic Sourcing is responsible for maintaining the whole structure created, managing the spending in each group of products.

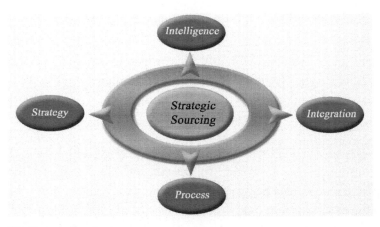

Figure 2-2: Strategic Sourcing key areas

It is not easy to define Strategic Sourcing since it affects so many different areas of a company, but in order to enable this initiative, a company should cover the following areas:

- **Intelligence** – A structure should be created focusing on the improvement of the knowledge of product, process, industry, and market.

- **Integration** – Strategic Sourcing should promote not only internal process integration, but also integration with external partners (e.g. suppliers, customers, associations, etc.)

- **Strategy** – Decisions should follow a well-defined strategy, which should be aligned with the goals of the organization and supported by the appropriate structure, processes, and tools.

- **Process** – The purchasing processes should be managed for compliance, and continuous improvement.

More than a simple reengineering of processes, Strategic Sourcing works towards the implementation of a new philosophy in the company. It makes people think not only about their immediate needs, but also about all the factors involved in a business decision. Different options are created and analyzed from a holistic point of view.

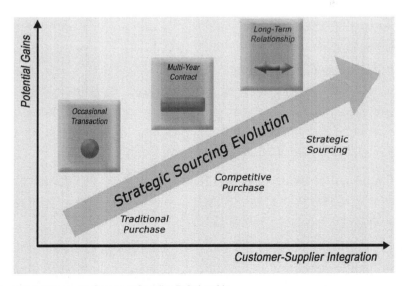

Figure 2-3: Stages of a Customer-Supplier Relationship

The relationship with the vendors is also strongly affected by the Strategic Sourcing concept. Figure 2-3 shows the different stages of this relationship. As the relationship with the supplier evolves, we can observe some clear differences in the way business are conducted.

In the <u>Traditional Purchase</u> stage, the relationship is based on occasional transactions or short-term contracts. The supplier has very little or no interaction with the final customer. Most of the time, the negotiation is basic, and price is the focus. The relationship works on a need to know basis.

In the <u>Competitive Purchase</u> stage, the company works with multi-year contracts. The communication with the supplier becomes more open, and limited information about forecasts and future plans is shared between the parties. Instead of focusing on price, the company starts focusing on cost reduction using the competition among different suppliers to achieve this goal.

The <u>Strategic Sourcing</u> company is very different from the Traditional Purchase one. Contracts represent long-term relationships. Information such as new product development, forecasts, and inventories is shared in real-time. It is also possible to observe the creation of multifunctional teams for specific projects involving the collaboration of suppliers. The supplier works with agreed performance and cost targets. After the necessary structures are put in place, the focus is on managing the spending.

After reading about what Strategic Sourcing is about and its importance, it is time to understand the implementation process. Maybe one of the most difficult steps towards Strategic Sourcing is to convince the organization of its importance and benefits. Strategic Sourcing has a broad scope, and it is not easy to think about all the impacts of this initiative.

Since Strategic Sourcing integrates the different areas of the company, it should not be seen only as a change in processes, but also as a change in philosophy and behavior.

The first step in the transformation of the company is to identify the key people in the organization (stakeholders) and educate them about Strategic

Sourcing. In addition, we have to show the stakeholders the potential benefits of such an initiative.

A Strategic Sourcing implementation may affect companies in different ways. The goals and opportunities of the project depend on the current status of the company's purchasing process, its relationship with suppliers, its characteristics of the industry, and many other factors. Therefore, some research will be required to prove the potential benefits.

Once the data is collected and analyzed, it will be possible to define the opportunities and prioritize them. A business case should demonstrate the benefits and savings of the Strategic Sourcing initiative.

In summary, the implementation of Strategic Sourcing is a difficult mission. Among other things, it involves gaining the support of many different people inside and outside the organization, collecting and analyzing a huge amount of data, implementing new tools and processes, being aware of possible changes in the market and in the organization, and creating new strategies for specific products.

Many companies have tried to implement Strategic Sourcing. Some of them have failed and some have succeeded. So, what is the trick? How to make things work smoothly? Start by listening to the ones who have already been there. Follow the best practices!

Chapter 3

Best Practices

"Everything has been said before, but since nobody listens we have to keep going back and beginning all over again"

Andre Gide

I remember, when I was 5 years old, hearing my parents telling me not to play with electrical outlets because I could get hurt. Despite of the warnings, and motivated by my curiosity, I stuck a key into an outlet and felt 110 volts running through my body. That is my oldest memory about how painful ignoring a best practice can be.

In *Men are from Mars, Women are from Venus*, Dr. Gray presents a series of common mistakes men and women make while relating to each other, and how to avoid them. Those are best practices that can improve the personal life of many couples.

In the same way, best practices are widely used in the business word. For example, consulting companies are specialists in best practices. In order to improve the skills and knowledge of the consultants, the companies build databases with information about the projects they did, tools they used, templates, charts, and presentations they created. In addition to their own material, their knowledge center also brings databases with information they buy from specialized companies.

Part of the consultant's time is dedicated to exploring those databases in search of articles, benchmarking studies, new trends, methodologies, and others. The collective knowledge available to the consultants allows them to quickly provide their clients the best solutions already tested in other projects. Consequently, they can avoid common mistakes and improve the chances of success of any project.

This chapter discusses some of the main lessons learned in different Strategic Sourcing projects. More than simple suggestions, these six practices are requirements for a successful project. The practices presented are:

- Leadership,
- Total Cost,
- Fact Based Analyses,
- Technology,
- Strategic Thinking, and
- Proper Communication.

3.1 - Leadership is Essential

Strategic Sourcing is a daily battle that demands a lot of effort from the entire company. Therefore, a strong and committed leadership is fundamental for the success of this initiative.

The leaders of the organization should understand the concept behind Strategic Sourcing. They should be aware of its cultural and organizational impacts. The leaders should fully support this initiative not only with words, but also with real actions. They should invest the Project Manager with the necessary power to implement the changes, and help him to eliminate any problems he might find in his way.

Sometimes, a leader is not successful in motivating his team even after following all the necessary procedures for Strategic Sourcing implementation. There is a difference between "Compliance" and "Commitment" that should be very clear in the mind of the executives. This is what differentiates a good professional from a great professional.

This difference can be observed everywhere. For instance, think about the kids parents send to piano classes. Some of them have great potential, but they have no interest in piano. They go to the classes and do everything that is required. They are complying, but they are not committed. Musicians that are not committed will never realize their full potential.

If at any moment the employees realize that the leaders are not fully committed to the project, the group may think they don't need to be committed either, and the project may never reach its full potential. Therefore, the Project Manager should keep track of the commitment level of the leaders. He should improve their motivation by including them in some of the main activities, periodically communicating to them the project status, and reminding them about the goals and benefits of Strategic Sourcing.

Remember that Strategic Sourcing is about implementing a cultural change in the company. Consequently, the Project Manager should give the proper attention to Change Management initiatives in all levels of the organization. He should promote Strategic Sourcing in every possible way to make everyone in the organization comfortable with the changes.

3.2 - Total Cost Rather Than Price

Price is not everything! This may be a though change for some buyers who are used to conducting aggressive negotiations in terms of price. Price will still be an important component of the equation, but not the only thing they should focus on.

Rather than price, the company has to consider the overall cost of the purchase. For example, perishable products may have higher handling or inventory costs than other kind of products. Some mechanical and electrical equipment may have higher maintenance or disposal costs. These "other" costs influence the economic performance of the purchase.

The buyer has to consider all the different costs an item may have along its useful life, and determine ways to drive these costs down. Some other factors besides the total cost may affect the purchase decision. Things like how well the equipment performs, how it fits in the overall strategy of the organization, current financial situation of the company, and others should be taken into consideration.

Besides the total purchasing cost, buyers may also consider the services related to the product - for example: the warranties, training, and customer service provided by the supplier. In addition, we can include here items such as how the supplier answers complaints, and whether it guarantees levels of performance (e.g. on-time delivery, damage-free products). These items may be harder to quantify, nevertheless they may represent an important component in the Total Cost of Purchasing.

The Total Cost of Purchasing, also known as Total Cost of Ownership considers all the costs from the moment of acquisition until the retirement of the product. This concept is one of the reasons why Strategic Sourcing must be considered not only from the perspective of a single department, but as the combined effort of the entire company.

Figure 3-1 shows some components of Total Cost of Purchasing. Note that this list is not comprehensive. New components may be added according to the item purchased and nature of the business.

Each product will present a different set of associated costs. Therefore, it is necessary to develop a cost model for each situation. The best companies in the market consider cost modeling to be an important purchasing skill.

The goal of any cost modeling is to understand how the purchase influences the company's results (e.g. Profit & Loss and Cash Flow). From the Cash Flow, it is possible to calculate many financial indicators in order to evaluate and compare different options. Some of the most common are Internal Rate of Return (IRR), Net Present Value (NPV), and Payback. In Chapter 12, we will analyze a mini-case focusing on these calculations.

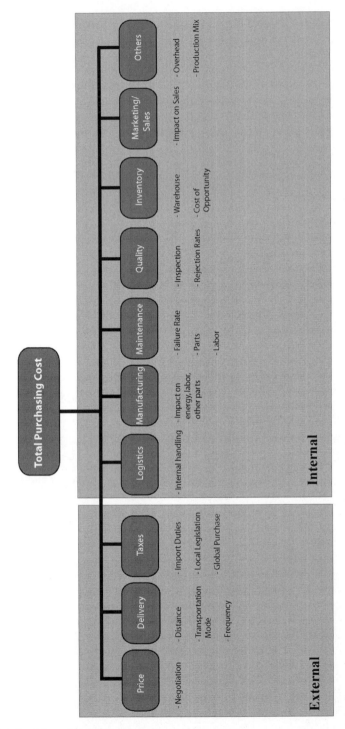

Figure 3-1: Total Cost of Purchasing Components.

3.3 - Strategic Sourcing is Fact Based

In the movie "Field of Dreams," Kevin Costner plays an Iowa corn farmer who, hearing voices, interprets them as a command to build a baseball diamond on his land. He builds the field, and the Chicago Black Sox come to play.

In the movie, only Kevin Costner could hear the voices. Because of that, many people didn't believe in him, and thought he was hallucinating. We can draw an analogy with real life here: If you have a plan, but you can't support your ideas with concrete data, you may lose credibility. Since Strategic Sourcing deals with different stakeholders and proposes so many changes in the company, credibility is very important.

That is the reason a professional in this area has to feel comfortable collecting and analyzing a large volume of data. Decisions in Strategic Sourcing are based on facts and numbers.

Most of the analyses in Strategic Sourcing try to anticipate the future and evaluate the outcome of possible courses of action. The accuracy of the results of these analyses will be directly related to the accuracy of the data used to prepare them.

Therefore, the group in charge of the analyses does not only try to capture as much information as possible about the company, processes, financials, patterns, customers, competitors, and others, but also challenges the quality of the data presented.

The collection and analysis of the data is not used just for identifying and evaluating opportunities. Strategic Sourcing also puts emphasis on the use of the data to track improvements.

The Strategic Sourcing team must be able to demonstrate its achievements. In order to do that, they need to define and measure key performance indicators affected by each initiative that Strategic Sourcing puts in place.

3.4 - Technology is your Friend

I still remember my first computer. It was one of the most popular home computers in the 80s. The CPU was a 3.58 MHz Z80 with 64Kb of memory. In other words, it was a little less powerful than many of today's most popular calculators.

The quick evolution of technology brought a world of possibilities for companies looking for improvements. However, some companies have not been able to explore the full potential of their Strategic Sourcing areas because they believe their current systems should be able to support all their new strategies. Therefore, they limit their development to the extent of their current technology.

Executives have to accept that new strategies may require not only a small improvement in the current systems of an organization, but a complete transformation.

Strategic Sourcing may utilize technology as a tool to enable initiatives that were not possible in the past. Every aspect of an organization can be improved through the combination of Strategic Sourcing and Technology.

Technology can greatly improve internal and external communication, ensuring that the right information will be available to the right person at the right time. New partners brought by Strategic Sourcing may imply an extension or transformation of the current communication channels.

By investing in new technologies, many large businesses reduce supply chain costs and streamline processes. Technology may facilitate tasks such as the requisitioning of goods and services, processing supplier invoices, creating complex Requests for Quotation (RFQ), negotiating contractual terms, and tabulating bidding results.

Strategic Sourcing may also utilize new technologies to improve visibility across the entire supply chain (e.g. tracking products, real time financials).

In addition, an efficient information system allows companies to maintain a good relationship with suppliers, sharing with them several important pieces of information, such as the status of their payment, the details of a specific order, updates regarding a bidding process, and others.

In conclusion, the necessary technology should be made available in a company implementing Strategic Sourcing; otherwise, they may not take full advantage of this initiative. The market is full of new technologies that, in the long run, can save millions for the companies and assure its survival.

3.5 - Be a Strategic Thinker

Another important skill for a professional in this area is achieving a strategic view. In other words, he/she should be able to see the big picture, understand different requirements, analyze the constraints, and propose effective solutions.

Most of the time, companies implementing Strategic Sourcing will develop partnerships and alliances. In order to do that, it is necessary to understand the requirements of the business and the characteristics of the prospective partner.

A good example of this strategic view comes from the purchasing group of one of the largest food companies in the world. This company has a pet food and a frozen dinner business.

The frozen dinner company was buying tons of chicken breasts, since it was one of the main ingredients of their dishes. However, their supplier did not know what to do with the rest of the chicken, and ended up charging them a lot more just because he had to look for another buyer for the other parts of the chicken.

The pet food company, on the other hand, could use the other parts of the chicken in their products. Therefore, these companies took advantage of their similar needs and saved millions of dollars by combining their purchases.

In conclusion, a company that may be in a different kind of business may be a great partner. Therefore, it is always necessary to see the big picture, think out of the box, and look for synergy opportunities.

Johnson & Johnson also knows what synergies are about. They have over 230 subsidiaries and operations in over 57 countries. J&J has experienced more than 70 years of consecutive sales growth, and more than 20 years of consecutive double-digit earnings increases.

These impressive results could not be reached just by doing the same things better. The only way they achieve what they have was by doing completely new things, and that is what they are doing.

J&J is always looking for synergies within their business models. Whenever one of J&J companies demonstrate excellence in one specific area, such as product development or purchasing of a particular item, J&J considers sharing this best practice among other segments of their business or even consolidating this function into a specific company.

A strategic thinker has the ability of planning for the future. The Strategic Sourcing professional should be able to understand the trends of the market and develop plans to assure the long term success of the company.

3.6 – Communication is Key

In the United States, approximately 1 million people file for divorce every year. In the beginning, those were good relationships, but at some point, something went wrong and the couples decided they would be better apart.

Many of the divorces happen because the partners fail to realize or to cope with the evolution in the relationship. Some evolution signs are very clear, such as winning the lottery, starting a new job, or having a baby. Other signs are not so obvious and demand more attention from both partners.

Sometimes, when couples cannot rationalize or pinpoint the problem, they look for a therapist or counselor. These professionals usually start by making explicit the needs, limitations, and expectations of the individuals. Only after understanding these factors, may the couple try to compromise and make some changes.

The basic philosophy is that if you do not recognize the problem, you cannot fix it. Specialists point to 'poor communication' as one of the main causes for divorces in United States. Only through good communication can couples understand the evolution in their relationships and change accordingly.

The same idea applies in the business world. Consultants substitute therapists in order to find the problems in organizations and suggest improvements. Good communication is their main tool to locate the problems. Peter Drucker illustrated this point very well when he said, "My greatest strength as a consultant is to be ignorant and to ask a few questions."

Being aware of the expectations in the relationship is the initial step for businesses to relate to each other. Therefore, good communication is essential in promoting the evolution of relationships.

In the first chapter, we saw how Lou Gerstner demonstrated how important his focus on communication was when he met personally with his business partners and customers to talk about the changes in IBM. Thanks to that, his business partners could understand the expectations of IBM and prepare their companies to cope with the changes.

Good communication gives the partners more time to react and adjust to the changes. Having bad communication with business partners is just like playing tennis with a brick wall instead of a net. We do not know what is going on beyond the wall, and we will have very little time to react after the ball crosses to our side of the court.

In *Men are from Mars, Women are from Venus*, Dr. Gray shown us some fundamental differences in the way men and women communicate. For example, one phrase coming from a man may be just a way to transmit a message, while the same phrase coming from a woman may be her way of reaching out for support. The reasons why is that Venusians and Martians communicate differently; therefore the expected actions resulting from this communication are also different.

Men and women may spend a lifetime living together and they will still misunderstand each other. In business we have to communicate by phone, e-mails, or with people we have never seen. The lack of personal contact and knowledge about our counterparts makes it harder to assure accuracy in our communication.

Communication is necessary along the entire Strategic Sourcing implementation. The implementation team will have to interact with the different areas, business partners, stakeholders, and assimilate information from different sources in order to deliver the best results for the project.

In summary, communication with business partners should be a top priority in the agenda of the executives. They should share their expectations, understand the position of their partners, and look for ways to consistently maintain good communication.

Section II
Implementation Process

Chapter 4

Strategic Sourcing Road Map

"The beginning is the most important part of the work."

Plato

Who doesn't have a friend who likes to play matchmaker? My friend Paula can make many cupids jealous. After graduating in Engineering in 1995, she opened her own matchmaking agency.

In the last 3 years, her agency brought together hundreds of happy couples. Her rate of success is outstanding. As much as 90% of the people who look for her services end up finding someone.

When I asked her what her secret was, she said "In the Engineering course we learned the art of analyzing and planning. After graduation I realized I could use my Engineering skills to build relationships instead of buildings. Nothing is impossible if we have a good plan and the right tools."

So, how to build successful relationships? Paula told me that the people looking for her services really have to be willing to commit. They should understand that looking for a relationship may be a tough process, so they should be willing to put a real effort in the process.

Paula first step is to run a series of tests in order to understand what her client wants and what he brings to the table. Based on this profiling exercise, Paula is able to create different options in order to find the best matches. The profile will tell her not only who she should be looking for, but also where to look.

Paula can take her clients to a night in the opera, a soccer game, a jazz bar, and even a rave party in order to find possible matches. She can also promote events such as theme parties or speed-dating, sending invitations to a target niche of the market. It is all about creating alternatives.

Paula's agency also offers a "Shape-up Program," where the clients receive tips on dating, develop their conversation skills, and improve some abilities, such as make-up, grooming, and fashion.

After exploring some of the alternatives and finding the right match, Paula does a follow up to evaluate if the relationship is sustainable and how to improve the chances of success.

In summary, Paula developed a well thought out plan in order to minimize the chances of failure. Her plan involves common business concepts such as understanding the product, defining a target audience, adapting the product to the audience, implementing the solution, and following up.

In Strategic Sourcing, we build relationships using an approach similar to the matchmakers. Every phase has a goal and every task a purpose. A good plan eliminates activities that do not add value. It ensures that all tasks link to each other in a smooth transition in order to minimize any issues.

Do not underestimate the importance of good planning. Thinking a few steps ahead may save millions of dollars in time and resources. Coordinated actions can give better results than isolated activities.

The implementation may be summarized in 6 phases. Figure 4-1 shows the Implementation Road Map highlighting the different phases and the main steps in each phase.

The duration of the project will depend on several factors such as the number of products involved, resources available, and complexity of the business.

Chapter 4 – Strategic Sourcing Road Map 43

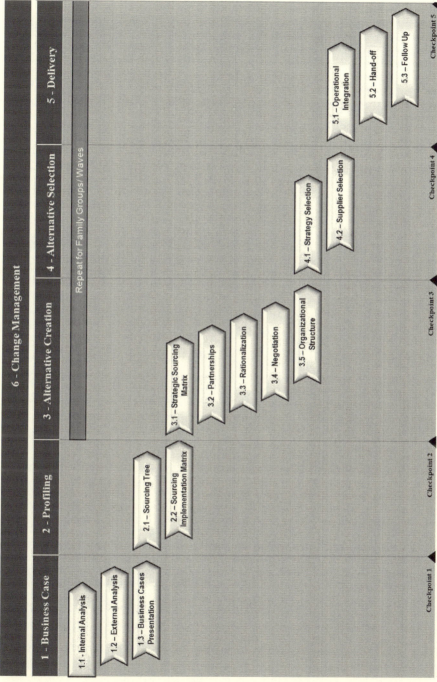

Figure 4-1: Strategic Sourcing Road Map

1 – BUSINESS CASE:

6 - Change Management				
1 - Business Case	2 - Profiling	3 - Alternative Creation	4 - Alternative Selection	5 - Delivery

The first step of the implementation is the Business Cases. In this phase, we will conduct a high-level assessment of the current situation and try to identify the main opportunities in Strategic Sourcing.

Have in mind that the opportunities will depend not only on the internal characteristics of the company, but also on the situation of the market. Therefore, the analyses in this phase are split into two main stages: Internal and External Analysis.

Besides gathering data and setting some preliminary targets, the goal of this phase is to educate the stakeholders about Strategic Sourcing, convince them about the importance of the project, and get their support and commitment for the next steps.

- **Checkpoint 1:**

The first checkpoint coincides with the Business Case presentation. At this time, a Steering Committee is formed to follow the progress of the implementation, and give appropriate guidance and support to the implementation team.

At this checkpoint, the implementation team looks for the approval of the Steering Committee on the project concept and implementation method.

2 - PROFILING:

Once the Strategic Sourcing implementation is approved, and the Sourcing Team is defined, the Profile phase may begin. Here, the team will analyze the company products, clients, vendors, channels, competitors, and every other variable that may affect the sourcing strategy. The idea is to have a good understanding of the environment and its variables in order to better identify and prioritize opportunities.

The products and services will be classified into different groups (Sourcing Tree) based on their characteristics. Next, we define the implementation priority of each group according to their characteristics and resources available.

The Sourcing Implementation Matrix will help the Sourcing Team to define implementation waves for the different groups of products and services. In other words, groups with higher priority will have a strategy defined and implemented before the team starts working with the lower priority groups in the next wave. Consequently, one of the main outputs of this phase is a detailed implementation schedule.

Most companies take from 6 to 12 months to implement the first wave, depending on their size and number of products. There is no rule for the number of waves or product families in each wave. The idea is to have a feasible schedule allowing good quality analyses.

- **Checkpoint 2:**

In the second checkpoint, the Sourcing Team should present to the Steering Committee the Sourcing Implementation Matrix and get their approval on the implementation schedule.

3 – ALTERNATIVE CREATION:

In the Alternative Creation Phase, the Sourcing Team will conduct some additional research to complement the information collected during the implementation in order to come up with possible sourcing alternatives for each group of materials and services.

The initial step in this stage is the creation of the Strategic Sourcing Matrix, which will guide the team to the most likely strategies to be implemented.

Next, the team should analyze the different possibilities in terms of partnerships, rationalization, negotiation, and changes in the organizational structure to ensure that the best solution is given for each group of materials and services.

- **Checkpoint 3:**

The role of the Steering Committee at this checkpoint is to ensure that the alternatives created are aligned with the overall strategy of the company. In addition, they should be sure that alternatives are feasible and coherent within the reality of the business.

The Steering Committee may ask for further studies for any specific strategy to ensure its feasibility.

4 – ALTERNATIVE SELECTION:

At the end of this phase, the Sourcing Team should have selected the best strategy, and defined the respective suppliers. The best strategy is selected based on the portfolio of suppliers and the requirements of the possible alternatives.

After defining the best strategy, the Sourcing Team will build a portfolio of possible suppliers based on a first qualification screening. The absence of qualified suppliers may require the Sourcing Team to step back and re-think the chosen strategy.

Next, the team will start a thorough analysis covering other factors that may play an important role in the selection process, such as the relationship with the supplier, its flexibility, and aggregated services they may provide.

- **Checkpoint 4:**

At this checkpoint, the Sourcing Team will present to the Steering Committee the selected strategy and suppliers. The alternative should be validated and approved by the Committee.

5 - DELIVERY:

6 - Change Management				
1 - Business Case	2 - Profiling	3 - Alternative Creation	4 - Alternative Selection	5 - Delivery

The Delivery Phase is divided in three main stages. First, we have the Operational Integration. This is the moment when the strategy is executed. The different areas of the company implement any necessary changes, and start to work with the new suppliers. This transition may be quite long, depending on the extension of the necessary changes in product and processes.

Next, we have the Hand-Off. In other words, the moment when the Sourcing Team transitions the responsibility of the daily operation to the areas involved with the project. For a short period, the Sourcing Team may closely follow the processes in what is called Assisted Operation in order to assure a successful transition.

Finally, the team moves to the Follow-Up activities. Some time after the implementation of the strategy, the Sourcing Team should review the results and compare them to what was initially planned. Based on this evaluation, the company can apply any corrective action and improve their process for the next waves.

- **Checkpoint 5:**

The last checkpoint does not seek for any particular approval or validation. The 5th checkpoint characterizes the end of the Strategic Sourcing implementation for the group of products and services analyzed.

The goal is to demonstrate the success of the project and increase the support of the stakeholders towards Strategic Sourcing. In addition, this checkpoint should also be used to share with the group the key lessons learned through the process.

6 – CHANGE MANAGEMENT:

6 - Change Management				
1 - Business Case	2 - Profiling	3 - Alternative Creation	4 - Alternative Selection	5 - Delivery

As seen in Figure 4-1, the Change Management Phase runs on a parallel track along the entire project. The reason for that is that for each step of the implementation there are many actions contributing to the acceptance and buy-in of the stakeholders.

Remember that Strategic Sourcing is a new philosophy that may bring many changes. Therefore, Change Management has to be included in the scope of any activity from the moment we sell the project until the final presentation in the Delivery Phase.

Chapter 5

Business Case

"Knowing a great deal is not the same as being smart; intelligence is not information alone but also judgment, the manner in which information is collected and used."

Dr. Carl Sagan

At the end of 2006, I was invited to attend a motivation seminar in Detroit. One of my favorite presentations was from a real estate agent. He was sharing with the audience some of the techniques that made him one of the best real estate agents in the US.

The first step in every new contact with a potential buyer was to develop a quick profile of the client. Basically, he wanted to understand who the person was, his job, hobbies, preferences, and any recent major transformations in life. For example, a new baby in the family which might indicate a preference for more space, safety, or a house close to good schools.

The reason for this initial screening was to understand the big picture. With some empathy, the agent would be able to put himself into the buyer's shoes. He would be able to understand his needs and main constraints in order to better advise him along the process.

According to the agent, understanding the big picture is 50% of the negotiation. The knowledge gained during this initial interview should be used as a reference for the rest of the sales process. It accelerates the search for the perfect house and allows the agent to help the client to identify what is really important to him.

Chapter 5 – Business Case

In the end, the real estate agent concluded that the initial assessment was the first sales opportunity. "It is like a first date. You have one chance to convince your date that you can be great together. In order to do that we explore common interests, show what we have to offer and that the relationship makes sense."

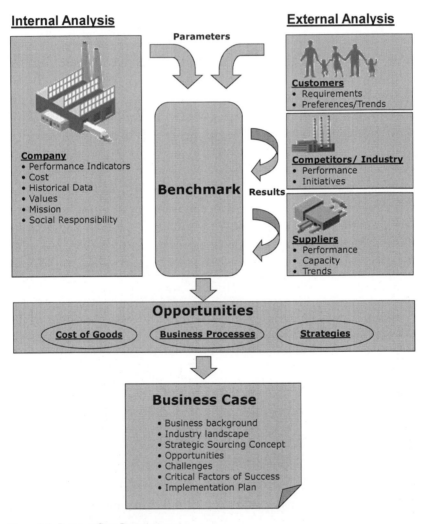

Figure 5-1: Business Case Preparation

In fact, that is what the Business Case is about. It is the first opportunity to sell Strategic Sourcing to the executives of the company and demonstrate all the potential benefits this initiative would bring to the organization.

During this phase, we will develop a Business Case, demonstrating how Strategic Sourcing can be used in the company. Furthermore, this initial study will allow us to have a better idea of the structure of the project, plan the necessary actions, and allocate the appropriate resources.

Remember that when we talk about Strategic Sourcing we are not just referring to an isolated action, but to many initiatives in different areas of the company. Therefore, in this phase we should analyze all the different areas involved.

The Business Case can be split in 3 main stages: Internal Analysis, External Analysis, and Opportunities. Figure 5-1 shows how these stages flow into the preparation of the Business Case.

The Business Case will show all the stakeholders where the company is situated in terms of Strategic Sourcing in relation to the market and the main competitors. Furthermore, it should educate everyone on the benefits of such implementation and how these gains can be achieved.

5.1 – Internal Analysis

This step focuses on all the internal processes and initiatives related to sourcing. The Internal Analysis will guide the internal opportunities. This analysis should give us information about Current Initiatives, Cost Drivers & Performance Metrics, and Company Identity.

a) Current Initiatives

The list of possible current initiatives impacting sourcing is usually long. Since this is a high level analysis, we avoid studying minor projects usually restricted to a specific area of the company. Therefore, we focus on major initiatives, such as Reengineering, Cost Reduction, Mergers & Acquisitions, Downsizing, and Organizational Changes.

52 📖 *Chapter 5 – Business Case*

At this point, we do not need to understand all the details behind these actions. However, we must be aware of their existence, and how they may affect any Strategic Sourcing implementation. Usually, quick interviews with those responsible for each initiative may give us all the answers we need in order to foresee any impact on Strategic Sourcing.

The key concern is to synchronize all the initiatives with Strategic Sourcing. Remember that many processes may be changing due to the current initiatives in the company. This may represent a challenge for Strategic Sourcing, since it may feel that many of the targets are currently on the move. Furthermore, these initiatives may compete for resources with Strategic Sourcing.

Here are some of the most common initiatives we can find while implementing Strategic Sourcing:

Reengineering - Instead of gradual improvements in the processes, Reengineering brings completely new processes and comprises a major break with the past. New areas, structures, and responsibilities may be created during this initiative. Depending on the scope of the Reengineering process, purchasing may be affected. The idea here is to understand the goal of the Reengineering and its impact on Strategic Sourcing actions.

Cost Reduction Programs - These are the most common type of initiatives. Cost reduction programs may focus on sustainable or temporary savings. Sustainable savings are usually related to changes in processes or materials used in order to achieve a more economical way to operate. Temporary savings involve actions to reach a particular target. Postponing projects and expenses are good examples of temporary savings initiatives. Strategic Sourcing initiatives may eventually collide with Cost Reduction Programs, since both of them may target savings through the rationalization of processes and products. Therefore, it may be necessary to coordinate the initiatives to avoid any kind of conflict and reach beneficial synergies by combining efforts.

Mergers & Acquisitions – Usually, one of the challenges in this kind of initiative is to combine different processes and cultural aspects from the companies involved. This duality in processes and mentality may represent an additional difficulty to the Strategic Sourcing implementation. In addition, some sourcing synergies may already be part of the scope of the merger or acquisition. Therefore, the Strategic Sourcing team has to coordinate its efforts with those responsible for the Mergers & Acquisitions initiative.

Downsizing and Organizational Changes – This is another very common type of initiative in companies looking for a slim structure. Downsizing and Organizational Changes may affect not only the headcount of the company, but also the internal relationship between its different areas. Strategic Sourcing initiatives should take into consideration the future design of the organization as well as any personnel requirements for the project.

b) Cost Drivers & Performance Metrics

Cost Drivers and Performance Metrics deal respectively with the financial and non-financial data that will allow the Sourcing Team to understand the current state and trend of the business or of a particular process.

Some common examples of Cost Drivers are value in inventory (finished products and raw material), cost of goods sold, expenses by business department, and earnings before interest and taxes. These numbers are found in the company's Income Statements, Cash Flows, Balance Sheets, and internal reports.

Performance Metrics, such as lead times, number of suppliers, number of products, late deliveries, shortages, and others, can be obtained from internal key performance indicator reports. Note that some of these indicators do not relate to the performance of the company, but to the performance of the suppliers.

The data collected should support Strategic Sourcing by:

- allowing a comparison between how well the company and its competitors are performing;
- highlighting critical areas of improvement;
- supporting the implementation of specific sourcing strategies;

54 📖 *Chapter 5 – Business Case*

- helping to estimate financial and operational targets for Strategic Sourcing; and

- allowing the implementation team to understand the main business processes and estimate the necessary resources to implement Strategic Sourcing in the organization.

In order to define the potential benefits of Strategic Sourcing, the team has to understand the evolution of the business. Therefore, the Sourcing Team analyzes the historical trend of the data collected. The executives of the company should be able to explain the main reasons for any variations, bringing up potential issues or initiatives already being implemented.

c) Company Identity

A company is more than its processes. Different factors interact to form the culture and define the values of a company. Among them, we have:

- Individual culture of the employees;

- Mission definition and social responsibility (usually defined upon the creation of the company);

- Relationship with Unions, and other non-governmental organizations; and

- Goals of the individual stakeholders.

One of the drivers to establish successful partnerships and guide the company in its strategy definition is the cultural aspects of the organization. Therefore, the elements above should be considered in order to fully understand the impact and opportunities of Strategic Sourcing.

5.2 – External Analysis

In 2005, I had the pleasure of attending a presentation at Domino's Pizza's headquarters in Ann Arbor, Michigan. David Brandon, the Domino's Pizza CEO, talked about his experience when he assumed the role in 1999.

In the first few days in his new position, David was surprised by the high headcount turnover at Domino's. David said the turnover was close to 150%, more than 10 times what he saw in the other industries he had worked in. In other words, every year it was necessary to hire and train 180,000 new employees.

When questioned about that number, the head of Human Resources told David that the high turnover was common in the pizza delivery business, and that Domino's was one of the best according to a recent benchmarking survey.

David thought that, maybe, they shouldn't compare Domino's to other pizza delivery businesses. That might lead them to maintain a model that was not good enough.

That was the start of David's crusade to bring the headcount turnover down at Domino's and, in fact, in a few years, Domino's turnover decreased by more than 30%.

The External Analysis stage of the Strategic Sourcing implementation focuses on the industry and market. However, as shown by David Brandon's example, we should maintain an open mind while thinking about benchmarking and research. Perhaps, focusing on our own industry is not the answer.

Having that in mind, we start the benchmarking phase in the Strategic Sourcing implementation by defining our research parameters (the information we expect to get from customers, suppliers, competitors, and other industries with similar processes.)

Part of the parameters was already defined during the Internal Analysis. They are the cost drivers and performance metrics. The other research parameters are defined according to the analysis of the customer preferences.

The Marketing department should be able to provide the requirements, preferences, and trends perceived among customers. For example, our target markets may require products with greater shelf life, a specific level of quality, a particular kind of package, or demonstrate a trend toward

56 □ Chapter 5 – Business Case

environmental friendly products. All these requirements may indicate new parameters to be taken into consideration during the benchmarking.

After defining the parameters, we can start the benchmarking study, but remember that taking as reference other companies that adopt similar business models may lead us to be the best of the players using a deficient model. Perhaps, it is necessary to increase the scope of our benchmarking by looking into slightly different industries and other geographical regions.

For instance, it is not unusual to see companies in the US changing their process based on the performance demonstrated by companies in Japan. The performance of our suppliers should be measured against results of the benchmarking in order to evaluate possible improvements.

Next, we analyze the performance of our main competitors. It is possible that much of the information needed will not be available. The sourcing team should try to obtain as much information as possible about the competitors in order to understand their sourcing initiatives, and how they translate into competitive advantages.

The External Analysis will also serve as support for the definition of possible strategic partnerships. Candidates for potential partners may be found among the company's competitors, buyers, suppliers, and substitute producers.

It is usually clear to the companies who their competitors, suppliers, and buyers are, and why alliances with them are important. However, many companies ignore substitutes as potential partners.

Substitutes are the companies commercializing the products our customers would buy if ours were not available. For example, if a soda is not available, customers could buy juice or water. Therefore, these companies may have similar processes and common interests. Agreements around the development of new products, distribution, and purchasing actions are not out of context.

5.3 – Opportunities

While the Internal Analysis gives us the main cost drivers and performance elements of the company, the External Analysis shows us how these indicators compare to the best in class.

Therefore, after those analyses, we should be able to identify the main opportunities and establish high-level goals for Strategic Sourcing.

The opportunities can be grouped into the following categories: Cost of Goods, Business Processes, and Sourcing Strategies.

5.3.1 – Cost of Goods

One of the most important components in Strategic Sourcing is the Cost of Goods. This indicator usually represents a good portion of the Income Statement, and can be described as the cost of the raw material, direct labor, and manufacturing processes.

By comparing the Cost of Goods of the company to the results of the Benchmarking, it is possible to find potential areas for improvement. Depending on the level of detail of the Benchmarking, it is possible to identify with more accuracy the items that need to be addressed.

For example, average consumption of raw material, cost of finished goods, depreciation of assets, and production cycle-time are a few of the many indicators that can help the company to identify improvements in materials, processes, and equipment.

Product redesign techniques may be suggested as part of the Business Cases in future phases of the project. These techniques analyze improvements, substitutions, or alterations in the specification of the products, and standardization of processes and parts.

It is strongly recommended to involve the suppliers in any product redesign process. They may be able to help the company to understand possible product alterations and bring additional knowledge about new trends and technologies available. Combining efforts with suppliers may significantly improve the quality of the results.

A simple example of savings opportunities in Cost of Goods is the possible reduction of the number of colors in a label. This simple alteration may reduce the final cost of the product.

Another example of opportunities may be found in the identification of trends among the customers. For instance, market research may identify a growing segment of the market for alkaline batteries willing to buy packages with more units per package than what is currently available in retail stores. This need may have been triggered by concerns about terrorism, hurricanes, and other disasters. Consequently, a change in the packaging size and its design may reduce the costs of transportation, material, and others.

5.3.2 – Business Processes

Opportunities in Business Processes may be identified by analyzing the performance indicators and overhead costs in the benchmarking. Remember that we are not talking only about the manufacturing process, but also about all the other processes impacted by purchasing.

A company with high costs in one specific area compared to the benchmarking results may indicate inefficiencies in the purchasing process or high usage of services and materials in that category.

Of course, the Sourcing Team should consider the size of the company and differences in their structure during these analyses. However, if the performance still looks unsatisfactory even after considering those factors, the Sourcing Team should work on the improvement of the process and rationalization of the volume purchased.

The improvement of the purchasing process and the rationalization of the volume purchased will be studied for each group of products by the Sourcing Team during the Strategic Sourcing implementation.

Some examples of changes in the purchasing process include: new bidding process, creation and maintenance of purchasing orders, changes in performance incentives, alterations in the length of contracts, and use of tools such as blanket orders.

In addition, the purchase process may also be affected with new e-commerce systems and the use of credit cards, p-cards, radio frequency tags, and other mechanisms.

Opportunities in Logistics, Marketing, Human Resources, and other areas will be analyzed in detail during the implementation according to the kind of material and services they purchase. Nevertheless, do not underestimate the potential savings in these areas. During the Strategic Sourcing implementation at Southern California Edison, an electric utility company, the redesign of the logistics processes generated $30 million in cost reduction. The changes involved a better coordination in the areas of transportation, job site delivery, and inventory strategies.

The group should also examine the business processes with a critical eye in order to discover whether a process adds value to the supply chain. The goal is to have more streamlined and effective processes.

Other opportunities for improvement are in the link between processes. By enhancing the internal communication and collaboration it is possible to improve the accuracy of planning, transparency in different processes, and the speed that data flows across different areas.

It is difficult to define and measure all the opportunities so early in the process. However, the goal for the Business Case is to obtain a ballpark number based on the results of the Internal and External Analyses to serve as a target or reference for possible savings.

5.3.3 – Sourcing Strategies

While the Cost of Goods brings opportunities related to manufacturing, and Business Processes analyzes the improvements in the support activities in the company, Sourcing Strategies deals with opportunities in the dynamics between the company and the market.

In order to create the best sourcing strategy for a company, it is necessary to understand the environment where it operates and its constraints. The

Internal and External Analyses should have most of the necessary information.

Looking into the existing relationships with the traditional suppliers, it is possible to find improvement opportunities. For example, many companies who started sharing their planning information became more flexible, reliable, economical, and able to carry smaller inventories along their entire supply chain.

It is also important to look into new partnerships. Possible agreements with different suppliers, buyers, competitors, and any other company sharing common interests should be evaluated.

For example, Hindustan Lever Limited (HLL) and ITC, two of the largest companies in India, are taking advantage of strategic partnerships. In 2006 they announced alliances with the Indian Railways in order to build a low cost model for transportation and storage. Among several advantages for all the companies involved, this partnership will allow them to recover part of the eleven billion dollars of fruit and vegetables that are lost every year due to inefficiencies in the supply chain.

The External Analysis and Benchmarking may show the results for outsourcing services currently used by the industry and other forms of partnerships. The sourcing team should analyze these results and evaluate whether the models used in the industry would suit their business requirements.

Creativity will play a major role in the definition of partnerships. In fact, even companies in different industries may have similar interests and, therefore, should be considered potential partners. A good example of this was presented in Chapter 3, where we showed the case of the Pet Food and a Frozen Dinner companies working together in order to achieve gains in the purchases of one of their main ingredients.

There are many possibilities a company can explore in terms of strategy. The correct definition of the opportunities will depend on the result of the Internal and External Analyses.

The opportunities described in the Business Case are usually based on traditional models already applied in the market. Because these models are currently in use, they represent lower risks and great potential savings. However, more innovative partnerships should be analyzed throughout the Strategic Sourcing implementation.

5.4 – Business Case Presentation

The Business Case is a preparation phase for the implementation. It is the transition point where all the stakeholders become more involved with the project, agreeing on the goals, and committing their support.

The results of this phase are usually presented to the main executives of the company. The Business Case usually starts with the current situation of the organization and an overview of the environment in which it operates (e.g. industry, competitors, suppliers, and other partners). It should also introduce the Strategic Sourcing concept, describing the main challenges and opportunities for improvement.

Another important part of this document is the description of the critical factors of success. These elements should be clearly presented, showing the stakeholders how to mitigate the risk of some of the challenges.

In 2005, I visited one of the biggest apparel companies in California, and had a chance to ask the Director of Strategic Sourcing what his main concern was when he presented the Strategic Sourcing Business Case for the stakeholders.

He told me that one of the critical factors of success of the project was to attract and maintain qualified professionals. When this company started their Strategic Sourcing implementation their competitors were already ahead in the game, so they would need people with a certain level of experience in developing this kind of role in order to accelerate the implementation. However, there were not a lot of professionals with experience in Strategic Sourcing available in the market.

After analyzing the Business Case and seeing all the opportunities for improvement, the stakeholders understood the request of the director, and authorized the new area to offer a compensation package above the market for professionals who fitted the required description.

In conclusion, the Business Case should be able to show not only the main benefits of the project, but also the main challenges. It should explain the Strategic Sourcing philosophy and demonstrate the main changes expected in the company.

Based on the Business Case, the stakeholders should decide if the company should invest their resources in this initiative. Once it is approved, they should elect champions in each area to support the Strategic Sourcing Team throughout the implementation.

Chapter 6

Profiling

"For every minute spent in organizing, an hour is earned."

Benjamin Franklin

The Business Case should have introduced the stakeholders to the concept of Strategic Sourcing, highlighted the importance of this initiative, and provided a sense of direction for the next steps. Above all, the Business Case should have ensured the commitment of the stakeholders.

The Profile Phase presents to the Sourcing Team a more detailed illustration of the company that will allow them to better understand and prioritize the opportunities.

Whether we are talking about business concepts or personal relationships, the development of a profile is always done to allow us to make quick and accurate decisions.

While in America, the process of getting to know each other usually entails to years of dating, in other countries like India, the process is streamlined through arranged marriages, a quite common event, even in today's India.

Although there are many different ways an arranged marriage can take place, the most common starts with the guardians of the groom or bride announcing that they are in the market for a committed relationship. Next, we may have a photo exchange, interviews, and background checks for both parties. In other words, every effort is made to ensure that the profiles of the groom and bride are accurate and will lead to the best decision.

In Strategic Sourcing, the Profiling Phase will be the foundation for all the upcoming phases of the project. Therefore, the sourcing team should invest the appropriate amount of time to understanding the main characteristics of the goods and services purchased, and classify these items into groups according to their features.

The correct identification of these groups, known as Sourcing Groups or Commodities Groups, will allow the Sourcing Team to develop strategies to better fit the profile of each group.

In summary, a Sourcing Group is defined as a collection of products or services with similar characteristics that are likely to be sourced from the same set of suppliers, using the same purchasing strategy. A company may have as many Sourcing Groups as necessary.

6.1 – Sourcing Tree

The first step to define the Sourcing Groups is to create a Sourcing Tree, which is a graphical representation of how the products/services are clustered.

A Sourcing Tree may have many levels and can be built in different ways to better reflect the reality of the company and facilitate the development of new sourcing strategies. Let us consider only a three level Sourcing Tree in order to demonstrate this tool.

The first level breaks the items into major groups, referred to as "Categories." A company may purchase items in the following categories: Direct Materials, Indirect Materials, Services, and Capital Expenditure.

Direct Materials are all items directly related to the final product of the company. They are the raw materials.

Indirect Materials are all the other items that are not part of the composition of the end product, such as maintenance, packaging, and office supplies.

Services includes all the work done by different suppliers which benefit our company. Common examples are security, maintenance, transportation, and legal.

Capital Expenditures are all purchases classified as fixed assets and intangibles. Examples of capital expenditures are: new plants, new production lines, and vehicles.

Each of these categories presents specific characteristics that will influence the purchasing process and requirements for the development of a sourcing strategy. For instance, the control mechanisms for volumes and costs are usually more accurate for Direct Materials since they will compose the cost of finished products.

Indirect materials are usually allocated among different areas. These allocations hinder the visibility of the process. In other words, Indirect Materials may require a different control mechanism in order to facilitate the understanding of their requirements and to track their usage.

Since the final destination of Direct Materials is the company's customer, the quality control and impact in case of failure are higher than in indirect materials and services. Consequently, direct materials should rely more on supply chain integration and the use of preferred suppliers.

"Families" are the second level of the Sourcing Tree. Families may be created based on the use, application, and composition of the items. Note that sub-families may appear as an additional level of the tree to improve the classification of the groups.

Families will usually be related to a specific market. For example, Figure 6-1 illustrates the concept of a Sourcing Tree with the Family "Plastics" defined under the "Direct Materials" category. Any changes in the "Plastic" market may impact all the products associated with this family.

In summary, having well defined Families facilitates actions and the usage of tools related to the coordination, control, and market intelligence of all the products related to this segment. For instance, changes in the resin price or a new legislation about plastic may affect every product in the Family "Plastics" in Figure 6-1.

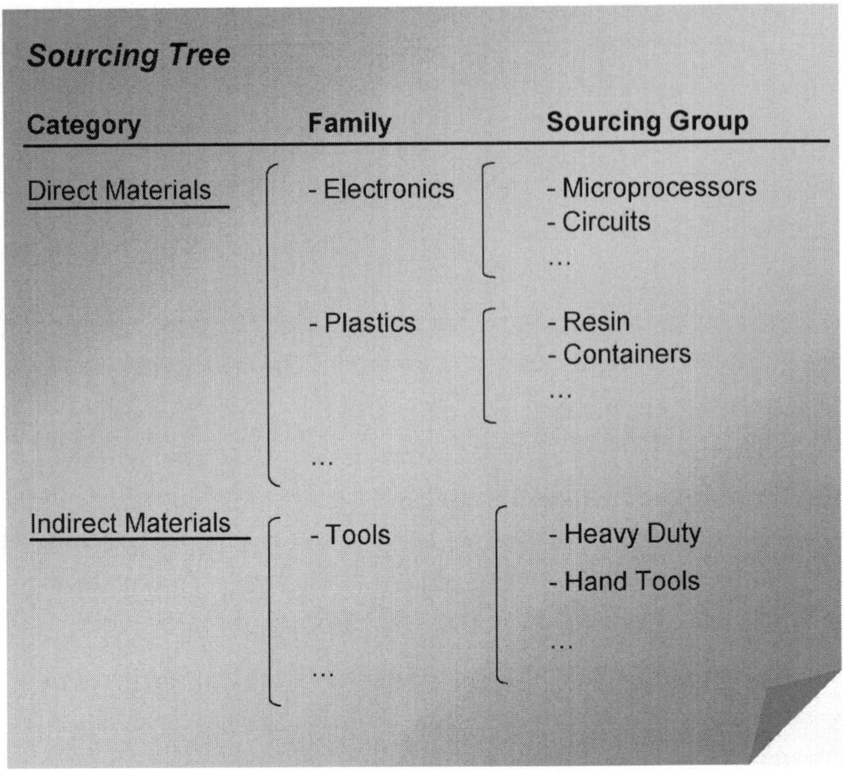

Chapter 6 - Profiling

Sourcing Tree

Category	Family	Sourcing Group
Direct Materials	- Electronics	- Microprocessors - Circuits ...
	- Plastics	- Resin - Containers ...
	...	
Indirect Materials	- Tools	- Heavy Duty - Hand Tools ...
	...	

Figure 6-1: Sourcing Tree Concept

At the final level of the Sourcing Tree, we will find the Sourcing Groups. As mentioned before, Sourcing Groups are likely to be sourced from the same set of suppliers, using the same purchasing strategy. They are usually defined based on their purpose, specifications, and technologies.

6.2 – The Sourcing Implementation Matrix

After defining the Sourcing Tree, companies may find dozens of different Sourcing Groups. In average, one Strategic Sourcing Manager can handle the implementation of 1 to 3 Sourcing Groups at the same time. The experience of many companies shows that it takes 6 to 9 months to process each Sourcing Group.

Consequently, it is necessary to prioritize the groups and break the implementation into different "waves." Each implementation wave will have a limited number of Sourcing Groups based on the resources available.

The priorities of the Sourcing Groups to be implemented are defined through the Sourcing Implementation Matrix (SIM). Figure 6-2 gives an example of this tool. The matrix takes into consideration the ease of implementing each group and the possible economical impact (savings) brought by the implementation.

Have in mind that in order to correctly address the savings and ease of implementation, it is important to "profile" each Sourcing Group. For example, the opportunities of savings for a particular Sourcing Group may not be feasible, depending on the market trends.

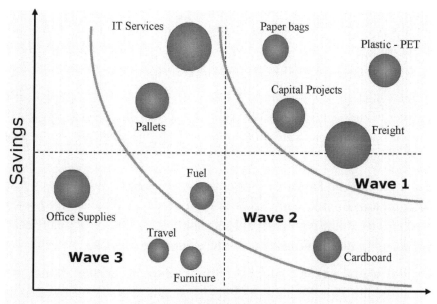

* The size of the circles represent the amount spent in each group.

Figure 6-2: Sourcing Implementation Matrix (SIM)

The profile of each Sourcing Group will bring important information, such as: total expenditure levels, volume purchased, function of the item, average price, channels utilized, relationship to strategic objectives, technical complexity, supplier alternatives, and any other piece of market intelligence collected in our Internal and External Analyses.

Savings are estimated based on the opportunities for improvements in each Sourcing Group. They should assume the Total Cost of Purchasing of the product or service. In other words, the savings along the entire life of the items in the Sourcing Group should be considered.

The ease of implementation is a less tangible concept than the savings. Therefore, it may be harder to be determined. However, it is possible to anticipate a more difficult implementation when the Sourcing Group presents some clear characteristics.

Items negotiated in complex or regulated markets usually present a higher degree of difficulty for their Strategic Sourcing implementation. In addition, items with high technological complexity also make the implementation harder, since the project may depend on the expertise of several specialists in order to decide on any changes.

Some Sourcing Groups will not present easy access to information. For instance, many companies with vendors that also supply products to the army may encounter some problem in verifying the production process of these suppliers.

Some of the Sourcing Groups may affect more areas in the company than other groups. Consequently, more stakeholders should be involved in the decisions regarding such groups. The number of stakeholders usually has a direct impact on the difficulty of implementing the solutions.

Finally, the geographic scope of the business is another factor that contributes to the difficulty. A Sourcing Group used in many different business units may have to be addressed on a local level. Therefore, the solution may be deployed into different parts, one for each geographical location.

Sourcing Groups with higher impact and ease of implementation should have higher priorities, and consequently, included in the first wave of implementation.

The first wave of Sourcing Groups will allow the Strategic Sourcing Teams to get used to the structure of the project, since their implementation is considered the least complex.

In addition, because of the high economical impact of the Sourcing Groups, the first wave should create a good momentum among the stakeholders, improving their commitment, and facilitating the assimilation of the new philosophy.

Also, have in mind that the profiles are dynamic due to changes in the market, new technologies, and other factors. Therefore, the Sourcing Team should constantly work to keep the Profiles updated.

Once the Profiles are completed, and the priorities are set, it is possible to define a detailed project schedule for the next phases of the Strategic Sourcing implementation.

Chapter 7
Alternative Creation

"Imagination is more important than knowledge."

Albert Einstein

In the matchmaking process described in Chapter 4, part of the plan was to create alternatives. Participating in different events and expanding the personal network allow any person to explore more options and maximize their chances of finding a perfect match.

In Strategic Sourcing, the team also wants to explore different options to find the best alternative. In this chapter, we present some of the main strategies utilized to improve sourcing initiatives. The first step in order to select the possible alternatives is to run the Strategic Sourcing Matrix (SSM).

This matrix helps identify the most likely strategy to be followed, based on the information gathered in the previous phases of the Strategic Sourcing implementation.

As we can see in Figure 7-1, the matrix is divided into 4 quadrants. The figure also brings some of the most common strategies associated with each quadrant.

The horizontal axis represents the complexity of the Sourcing Groups. High complexity items are those difficult to be reproduced or developed in-house. The complexity is associated to the technical knowledge required, and availability of the item on the market. Consequently, monopolistic, closed markets, or those with high entrance barriers (e.g.

high need of investments, proprietary technology, switching costs) usually indicate high complexity items.

Very often, the level of complexity is directly related to the market competition among the suppliers. A highly competitive market is a sign of a low complexity item or a market with a small number of buyers.

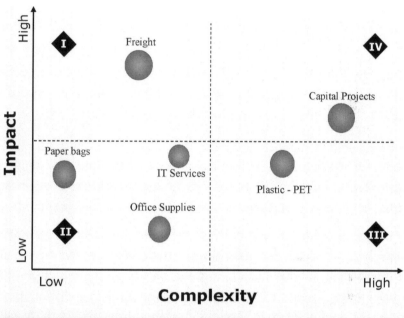

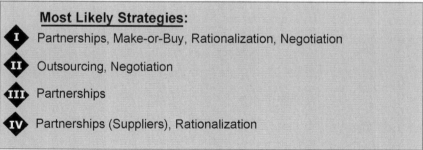

Figure 7-1: Strategic Sourcing Matrix (SSM)

Note that the power between supplier and buyer can shift according to the relative importance of the buyer. Even if the item negotiated is considered complex and presents only a few qualified suppliers in the market, the buyer may still have some negotiation power, provided that he represents a high percentage of the supplier's sales. A good example of this is the relationship between Dell and Intel. Although Intel microchips are very complex items, Dell still has some negotiation power due to the volume they purchase from Intel.

The availability of suppliers in the market is usually limited for items of high complexity. Consequently, suppliers often have a great advantage in the negotiations. Common strategies for these items involve the rationalization of products and processes, and the supply chain integration through alliances. The correct execution of these kinds of strategies can give an important competitive advantage to the company, since it will ensure the supply of strategic items.

Items or services of low complexity may be seeing as commodities, since it is easier to find suppliers for these items. Therefore, buyers have the advantage in this scenario. The greater the volume negotiated, the higher is the negotiation power of the buyer. Hence, options such as outsourcing, make-or-buy analyses, and demand consolidation are usually preferred.

The vertical axis of the matrix represents the Impact of the Sourcing Groups on the business. The impact is composed by two main components: the internal impact, and the impact on the customer. The internal impact is measured by the amount spent on the purchasing of the items in the Sourcing Group. Items with higher expenditures are usually closely controlled by the company. Variations in price may have a big impact on the operational result of the business.

Items with high impact on the customer are those which can help to differentiate the final product from that of the competition. It is the component or service that, in the eyes of the customer, adds value to the product. The failure or absence of these items could cause a negative impact on sales.

Items with high impact are controlled more closely by the company. Since small variations in price and quality can greatly affect the result of the company. The strategy for these items will usually focus on the reduction of the impact through rationalization techniques, and the study of possible partnerships.

Low complexity items with low impact on the business (Quadrant II of the SSM) tend to be outsourced whenever possible. For low impact items with high complexity (Quadrant III of the SSM), the focus is to ensure the supply by working on the relationship with the vendors.

Certain categories of Sourcing Groups are more likely to fall in specific quadrants of the Strategic Sourcing Matrix. For example, direct materials usually have a high impact on the business. They can be complex or not depending on the nature of the product. In addition, direct materials are usually negotiated in great volumes, giving significant power to the buyer over the suppliers.

Remember that the Strategic Sourcing Matrix in Figure 7-1 presents the strategies that are most likely to be followed. Many other factors may influence the possible alternatives. Therefore, it is important to consider all the information collected during the Business Case and Profiling Phases.

As mentioned in the Internal Analysis in Chapter 5, other initiatives in the company (e.g. Reengineering, Downsizing, and Mergers) can affect the alternatives and should be taken into consideration.

The mindset of the organization and its stakeholders will also restrict some of the options. For instance, companies willing to be first adopters of new technologies may face higher risks, but are able to explore a greater variety of strategies.

The alternatives for each Sourcing Group should be aligned to the company's overall strategy. The Marketing Strategy may focus on a new product, or the development of a particular brand, geographic region, or other demographics. Consequently, the Sourcing Strategy should support these goals.

As you can see, there is no easy way to define the right alternatives for each Sourcing Group. The knowledge base created throughout the project should be completely evaluated and understood in order to guide the team through the possibilities. In order to simplify our understanding of the main strategies, we split them into four categories:

74 📖 *Chapter 7 – Alternative Creation*

- Partnerships,
- Rationalization
- Negotiation, and
- Organizational Structure

7.1 – Partnerships

Partnerships may be structured in many different ways. Here, we will exemplify some of the main kinds of partnerships the sourcing team may consider. They can range from an agreement with very limited scope to the complete acquisition of the partner.

7.1.1 – Vertical Integration

In Strategic Sourcing, we focus on the upstream integration of the Supply Chain (suppliers). Therefore, this kind of integration, also referred to as "Backward Vertical Integration," deals with the joint-ventures, mergers, or acquisitions of suppliers.

In these kinds of agreements, the buyer gains partial or total control over the supplier. Consequently, it enables the buyer to capture upstream profits, and achieve savings due to synergies with the supplier.

Three of the most common savings in this kind of strategy are:

- Lower transaction costs by achieving synergies in the processes;
- Lower inventories along the supply chain through the synchronization of supply and demand;
- Better control of quality issues.

These savings can be reflected on the final product, increasing the competitiveness of the business, and creating barriers for new entrants.

For example, in the 20's, it was a common practice for the car manufacturers to own tire, glass, and metal companies. This structure created a barrier for new manufacturers to come into this market, since competitors not vertically integrated would not be able to compete in price.

Vertical Integration is more often applied to complex Sourcing Groups (Quadrants III and IV of the SSM), since in these groups the buyer usually has less power, and the negotiations can be tougher. In other words, if the suppliers are too powerful, it might be a good idea to buy some of them.

Of course, Vertical Integration has many risks and downsides. One of the most common is the "technological freeze." In a vertically integrated company it is common to see the supplier reducing its technological development pace, since they experience a lower level of competition.

Consequently, a few years after the integration, they may not be able to contribute to the business as much as external suppliers would. That is one of the main reasons why many companies are experiencing a "Vertical Disintegration."

Vertical Integration can be a very painful experience for all parties. Therefore, this kind of option should be analyzed with the help of professionals who are used to this kind of study. Before forming an opinion, consultants will verify several points. Just to name a few, they will analyze:

- Similarities between the core competencies of the buyer and the supplier;

- Financial health and legal situation of both companies;

- Potential synergies and savings;

- Extensive market analyses;

- Potential risks; and

- Cultural aspects (management style, internal policies, communication, career development).

Another way to improve the degree of vertical integration is by producing internally some of the items used as raw material. In other words, by eliminating a first tier supplier and dealing directly with the second-tier.

Let us take the example of Kitcharm, one small textile company in Brazil, which produces children's clothes. The basic production process in this kind of business is to get the fabric, cut, sew, and pack it. Back in the 80s, when this business started, Kitcharm realized they would not be able to compete against other companies that were already established in this market.

Kitcharm decided to compete in design and price. In order to do that, they changed their basic production flow. They decided to decompose the fabric into subcomponents and achieve savings by coordinating the production of their own fabric. In other words, they increased their vertical integration degree by going straight to their second tier suppliers.

Instead of buying the fabric ready to be cut, Kitcharm started the process by purchasing the thread. This thread was then taken to another vendor who would produce the raw fabric. Next, Kitcharm had to take the raw fabric to be dyed by another vendor. Finally, the fabric was taken to a fourth vendor who would stamp it.

The savings associated with this new process were more than enough to cover the additional steps. In addition, by deciding on the fabric color, and stamp patterns, they were not subject to the existing fabric available in the market. Therefore, they were free to create and set their own quality standards along the supply chain to best attend to the requirements of their customers.

Once again, remember that this kind of decision involves many different considerations, such as risks, savings opportunities, the existence of the necessary capability to produce the item internally, and many others.

7.1.2 – Strategic Alliances

Strategic Alliances are partnerships that explore long-term interests of the participants. The agreements do not cause any changes in terms of equity, so the integration should be a cooperative agreement between different companies.

The first step to create a Strategic Alliance for a specific Sourcing Group is to consider all the possible partners. By that, we mean Customers, Suppliers (all tiers), New Entrants, Competitors, and Substitutes.

Although these partners should have already been identified in the Business Case Phase during the External Analysis, this is a good moment to re-evaluate this list.

Each type of partner may present synergies in one or more specific areas. Here are some examples of possible Strategic Alliances:

a) Suppliers/ Customers

Alliances with suppliers are the most common. Companies try to develop long-term relationships and look for integration in order to reduce operational costs.

One good example of this kind of initiative is a technique called Collaborative Planning Forecasting and Replenishment (CPFR), also known simply as Collaborative Forecasting. It consists in establishing a continual line of communication between the buyer and the customers, predicting the future needs for raw material.

As the company's production schedule is developed, the vendors are alerted about the specific quantity of each product to be supplied. Better planning along the supply chain allows the suppliers to reduce inventories and other operational costs.

In 2002, Whirlpool installed a new CPFR system for sharing and combining the sales forecasts of its major clients - Sears, Roebuck and Co., Lowe's, and Best Buy Co. As a result, CPFR reduced forecasting

Chapter 7 – Alternative Creation

errors by 50%, allowing a reduction of finished-goods inventory by more than 20%, and a decrease of 5% in freight and warehouse costs.

Vendor Managed Inventory (VMI) is another common practice in the market. VMI is a form of consignment, where the supplier places the goods at customer location, executing inventory decisions about these items on behalf of the customer. The supplier owns the inventory until the point of usage by the customer.

By using Vendor Managed Inventory, ABB Robotics Division in Michigan experienced savings in overhead, working capital (cash outs are delayed until inventories are used), and $2 million in annual productivity savings among other favorable results.

Alliances with suppliers may impact many different areas. As we could see, CPFR and VMI can affect costs mainly associated with inventory and planning activities. However, we can also have alliances with suppliers affecting cost of production, sales activities, logistics, and other factors.

An example of alliances with suppliers to reduce advertising costs can be easily observed in supermarkets. Supermarkets allow certain suppliers to conduct marketing activities in their stores to increase the sales of products. Therefore, through these agreements, supermarkets reduce their advertisement efforts, and improve their sales.

The same kind of alliances made with suppliers to reduce costs may also apply to customers. Techniques such as CPFR or VMI, can bring better results to both partners.

Another popular supplier-customer partnership is Outsourcing. The goal of the outsourcing process is to eliminate the overhead cost for purchasing, execution, and control of non-core competencies of the company.

In other words, it applies to Sourcing Groups with low impact and low complexity (Quadrant II of the SSM). Usually, mature products and commodities are the majority of the items in this category.

Since these items are considered of low-complexity, the supplier market will most likely be competitive in price. Consequently, the buyer also has the advantage in the negotiation.

In contrast with other forms of alliances, outsourcing contracts are usually short-term oriented in order to maintain the pressure on the supplier to compete on price and look for improvements. However, as the relationship evolves, these contracts can also become long term commitments with targets for productivity and improvements.

The nature and scope of the agreements should be analyzed case by case. Although we named here a few examples, there is no simple answer to the question of which kind of agreement a company should pursue.

b) Substitutes/ Competitors:

The most common alliances made with competitors and substitutes involve Demand Aggregation. In other words, the companies combine their purchase power in order to increase their negotiation advantage over the suppliers.

Other agreements may focus on different areas, such as combined efforts to research new technologies. The goal is to look for mutually benefitial projects.

c) Other Businesses

Companies are used to considering alliances only within their own environment (e.g. customers, suppliers, and competitors). However, they should remember that the market always brings different opportunities for those with an open mind.

It is also possible to form strategic alliances with non-correlated businesses. In Chapter 3, we saw the example of the Pet Food and the Frozen Dinner companies combining their purchasing needs in order to improve their negotiations with the suppliers.

A newspaper company in South America came up with a creative solution to reduce their logistics costs. Every morning, they had to deliver newspapers to hundreds of stands and stores before 5AM. After that, their delivery trucks would not be utilized until next day. The idea was to make agreements with moving companies and other delivery services in order to improve the utilization of the trucks. By allowing these partners to use the vehicles for the rest of the day, the newspaper company saw a drastic reduction on its distribution overhead.

Cement companies also have interesting agreements in place. The oven to produce cement is one of the most powerful in the world. It can reach one third of the temperature of the surface of the Sun. Therefore, instead of using coal and other traditional sources of energy to maintain the heat, many cement companies are moving to alternate fuels.

Cement companies can safely use their ovens to burn used tires, diapers, and other undesired products from different industries. These actions reduce the energy consumption of the oven, and the disposal cost of the organizations providing these alternate fuels.

A Joint Sales initiative is another method that allows companies to achieve better results and reduce costs in commercial activities. For instance, Dynaloy LLC and BASF AG announced in 2007 a sales and distribution agreement for some specific products. The agreement enriches BASF's product portfolio for the semiconductor industry and gives Dynaloy access to key markets in Asia and Europe. Without this agreement, Dynaloy would have higher costs to penetrate these markets.

Some companies also try to make high complexity Sourcing Groups more popular by developing new entrants. More companies producing similar items leads to an increase in the buyer's purchasing power.

However, this strategy is not usually followed by high impact Sourcing Groups, because it may decrease the barriers for competitors causing a negative impact for the buyer's own business.

7.2 – Rationalization

The Rationalization of products and processes is usually not lead by the Strategic Sourcing Team. This task is often left to the managers of the different departments of the company. The problem with this approach is that, in many cases, the managers may not follow a methodical approach for improvements, and fail to work on the integration with other areas.

The Strategic Sourcing Team should lead or provide close support to these initiatives. They should involve champions from all affected departments, so that the processes and products can be analyzed from a holistic perspective.

Rationalization refers not only to the redesign of the product or service provided by the company, but also to the improvement of the production process itself. By changing the production process or the product, it is possible to influence the material requirements and achieve tremendous savings in procurement.

One option in the rationalization process is to optimize the specifications of the product being delivered to the final customer. This includes the standardization of materials, the use of substitutes, and the elimination of components and steps that do not add value in the production process.

There are many ways to execute this kind of study. We can go from simple techniques, such as Brainstorm, to complex exercises, such as Value Engineering Analysis (VEA), or a Quality Function Deployment (QFD).

In a nutshell, QFD is a technique used to translate the preferences of the customers into engineering requirements, and VEAs propose design alternatives based on the cost of these preferences. For example, if a customer prefers a self-cleaning oven, the QFD will transform this characteristic into a detailed engineering specification. A VEA will analyze the cost of each one of the customer's preferences and propose an economically acceptable alternative.

Have in mind that the changes made to the products are usually based on the opinion of the customers and evaluated through focus group sessions, marketing tests, and other sources of information that allow the company to better understand the acceptance of the new concept.

Joint Design Process is another strategy utilized by some companies where suppliers share the new product design initiatives early in the creation process. The most common example comes from the auto industry, where suppliers and customers work together in the designing of new cars. This strategy has many benefits, such as:

- Time-to-market speed - Products will be available sooner to the final customer. Generally speaking, companies that move first into a new market may have an advantage in establishing a better market share. From a financial point of view, this will also improve the return of the project.

- Better overall quality - The final product will have a better overall quality since the suppliers were involved since the beginning of the project, being able to analyze the impact of their component on the final product. This will also reduce future maintenance costs.

- General cost reduction - Since the suppliers were involved from the beginning of the project, it is possible to come up in advance with an optimal production plan, and also adjust their components to allow the most economical assembling method for the final product.

The Rationalization can also affect productivity and efficiencies by improving the processes. For example, the use of automation can speed up some repetitive tasks and greatly reduce the cost of the operations.

Techniques such as Just in Time (JIT) can optimize inventories, minimize work-in-process, and reduce stock outs. Radio Frequency Identification tools (RFID) may speed up the localization and identification of products during storage and transportation.

As we can see, there are many available techniques and tools to redesign products and processes. However, remember that for all of them, it is always important to consider the opinions of different specialists, such as designers, engineers, marketing/sales associates, the executives of the company, and the impact on the end-customer.

In order to exemplify the power of rationalization, let us take Nestlé Waters North America as an example. Nestlé Waters is the industry leader in sales of spring water in the United States. For two years the company has worked with their suppliers in the redesign of one of their most popular packages: the 0.5 liter bottle.

In 2007, Nestlé started the commercialization of a new 0.5 liter bottle, which requires a smaller quantity of raw material and offers the same structural integrity as the previous bottle. This result translates into millions of dollars in savings by cutting 35%, or 240 million pounds of the plastic resin per year. On top of that, the new bottle requires 20% less energy in the manufacturing process.

Nestlé Waters also uses this project to set an example for other companies. According to its CEO, Kim Jeffery, Nestlé wants to be "the leader in reducing their environmental footprint."

7.3 – Negotiation

As we mentioned before, odds are that the buyer will have the advantage in the negotiations with suppliers for items in highly competitive markets. Since these markets are usually formed by low complexity items (Quadrants I and II of the Strategic Sourcing Matrix), negotiation strategies may be responsible for great part of the savings in the project.

In order to improve the buyer's leverage, the company may look for a demand consolidation strategy. This consolidation may be done in different ways, such as through the reduction of the number of suppliers, consolidation of the demand of different partners, and consolidation of the demand across categories.

Each alternative is associated with different risks and opportunities. The reduction of the number of suppliers may simplify the standardization of processes and parts, and facilitate the communication and coordination with the suppliers. However, by depending on fewer suppliers, the company may increase its risk, since any issue with a vendor may have a bigger impact on the organization.

The second alternative, consolidation of the demand of different partners, refers to similar needs of different areas or companies. These partners can look for economies of scale and greater bargain power by consolidating their demand.

In addition, this alternative may be applied at different levels of the business. For example, let us assume that one factory ships different products through different carriers. At the factory level, we can consolidate all the different products produced at this factory and have them shipped through the same carrier. A consolidation at a geographical level could assume that all the different factories belonging to that company could use the same carrier. Finally, at the group level, we could propose that all the different companies of the group should use the same carrier.

The third option, consolidation of the demand across categories, refers to items from different Sourcing Groups that can be purchased from the same supplier. If the total value of the transaction with a specific supplier increases, he may be more willing to offer a better deal in order to retain the customer.

Negotiation strategies will also include tools and process to reduce the price of the products and services purchased. Electronic catalogues and reverse auctions are simple examples of these tools.

The extension of the contract terms may also help with reducing the total cost of the purchase. Longer terms may reduce the uncertainty and create a stronger relationship between the customer and the supplier.

Contracts with variable components may represent a risk to the customer, and should be managed accordingly. For instance, a transportation contract where the price is adjusted based on the price of the oil in the international market may represent a great risk for the customer. However, this could be managed by using financial instruments, such as hedges and option contracts.

Note that we have not mentioned any particular negotiation technique. The focus of these strategies is to improve the leverage of the organization. This work should be done prior to the negotiation in order to maximize the opportunities during the conversation with the partners.

7.4 – Organizational Structure

The company may operate under a centralized, decentralized, global, or local structure. Each decision presents pros and cons, and affects the kind of partners the company seeks.

There are many advantages in pursuing global suppliers. Each day more companies are realizing the potential in this strategy. Here are some favorable points we should consider:

- Lower Costs – Global suppliers may have a different cost structure due to different social-economic conditions at their production sites, proximity to sources of raw material, and other factors. The savings may be reflected in the overheads, material, energy, labor, taxes, or others.

- Quality Standards – Due to international regulations for exportation, some suppliers may offer higher levels of product quality.

- Specialized Items – Some regions in the world concentrate the commerce of specialized products and services. This may create economies of scale in that region and even the existence of a market with exclusive items.

- Availability of Supply – International suppliers may have excess production capacity. Therefore, by reaching these suppliers, a company may access a product originally limited in their own market, and improve their negotiation position with local suppliers.

It is possible to find many advantages in global suppliers, but we must not forget about the downside of this strategy. The savings due to lower production costs may be offset by logistics, tariffs, duties, and exchange rate fluctuations just to name a few.

Cultural differences may also be challenging in this process. For example, the language barrier, use of different units of measurement, and time difference may affect any technical support.

The distance from the suppliers may also increase the lead-time, and consequently, create more pipeline inventory. This also may have a negative effect on the returns and repairing of defective products. Companies abroad may be less responsiveness to help fixing problems.

Finally, socioeconomic, and political instabilities may represent a risk to maintain international agreements.

86 📖 *Chapter 7 – Alternative Creation*

Consequently, all these aspects and risks should be evaluated before a company engages into a global sourcing environment. Due to the level of difficulty in implementing this strategy, it will usually apply to high impact and high complexity Sourcing Groups (Quadrant IV of the Strategic Sourcing Matrix).

As for deciding on a centralized or decentralized purchasing structure, the Sourcing Team should evaluate all the trade-offs. Planning and purchasing decisions taken at a regional level (decentralized) may bring greater flexibility, shorter lead times, and quicker responses for any request made to the suppliers.

However, this scenario may also lead to a higher number of transactions with different processes and outputs. Therefore, it may be difficult to put in place mechanisms to track and control all the decentralized decisions.

Consequently, the Sourcing Team must be sure that the structure proposed is manageable, cost effective, and does not put the final products at risk in terms of quality.

Chapter 8
Alternative Selection

"It is not enough to have a good mind; the main thing is to use it well."

Rene Descartes

Selecting the best alternative in an environment full of uncertainties may be a very difficult job. My friend used to ask her mom how to know if a relationship would work. How could she tell if that was the man she should marry?

In her infinite wisdom, her mom came up with a simple formula: "Take all the things you don't like about him and multiply them by 3. If you can still see yourself married with this person after that, then the relationship has a chance."

I don't know if that works, but I loved the fact that she was trying to rationalize an emotional decision, quantifying and transforming it into a more rational approach. Decisions are easier when we have a set of tangible and well defined criteria.

In Strategic Sourcing there are many factors influencing the selection of the best strategies. These decisions should be made based on a logical and thorough analysis of the variables. The Sourcing Team should consider the potential savings, sustainability, and feasibility of the different strategies.

Some of the alternatives will not be feasible if the market is not able to present qualified suppliers. Therefore, an important task during the Alternative Selection is to evaluate and define the suppliers who may be supporting our business.

During the Alternative Creation Phase, the Sourcing Team came up with a list of possible partners and suppliers. This list will be evaluated against a qualification criteria defined based on the supply needs of the company.

The qualification analysis also includes the evaluation of the relationship with the existing supplier. The qualification criteria should be incorporated into a scorecard including both price and non-price factors (e.g. reputation, size, global/local, technology, capability).

This evaluation should result in a short list of qualified partners. After that, the next step will be the negotiation with the finalists in order to maximize the saving opportunities. Figure 8-1 shows the evolution of the Supplier Portfolio.

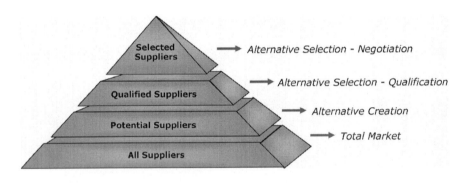

Figure 8-1: Supplier Portfolio Evolution

8.1 – Strategy Selection

The alternative selection starts by analyzing all the options brought up during the Alternative Creation phase. Each alternative should go through a critical evaluation of its feasibility and sustainability over time.

The overall goals of the possible partners, their willingness to cooperate, and their capacity to interact are critical factors in this evaluation. RFIs (Request for Information) may be sent by the Sourcing Team in order to obtain some of this information. In addition, depending on the kind of partnership the company is looking for, the team may try to contact directly the key people in the organization of the prospective partner (e.g. managers, directors, owners).

It is important to remember that there is always a risk component associated with each new strategy. The risk analysis is part of the strategy's feasibility study. This analysis may involve market projections, performance of suppliers, new technologies, and other factors.

After eliminating the strategies that are not feasible or sustainable due to the high risks or incompatibility of the possible partners in the market, it is necessary to analyze the remaining strategies from the cost perspective.

As mentioned before, the Sourcing Team should use the Total Cost approach in order to compare the different alternatives and decide on the strategies to be implemented.

8.2 – Supplier Selection

Like many other people in South America, I have grown up watching my mother following her favorite soap operas on TV. These shows are usually very predictable since their plot focuses heavily on family, personal relationships, emotional conflicts, moral dilemmas, and dramas.

Very frequently, the plot shows the good girl falling for the villain. Every time that happened I could hear my mother asking "Why does she put herself in that situation? Why does she trust such a bad person? Why does she insist on a relationship that leads nowhere?"

With those words, my mother just summarized some basic principles applied to successful commercial relationships. Poorly thought-out partnerships can be more detrimental than beneficial. In many cases, the problem in the soap operas is that the good girl trusts the villain. In the business world, trust is not enough for a relationship, but lack of trust will surely prevent the kind of collaboration that produces advantages.

While selecting a partner, the Sourcing Team should be sure that the relationship will be good for both sides. The team should develop a plan to implement and maintain the relationship. Effective relationships are built on common goals and are sustained through extensive two-way communication discussing performance and expectations.

Consequently, it is necessary to develop a deep knowledge of the supplier in order to understand its capabilities, plans, expectations, and make sure it qualifies as a partner.

There are many different ways to evaluate a supplier, such as surveys, technical visits, references from its customers, and others. Supplier Ratings are among the most common forms of evaluation. Basically, weights are assigned to different performance criteria, allowing the comparison between different suppliers.

Although the weighted average of the ratings can show the best qualified suppliers, it is also necessary to analyze each performance item separately, since there may be some required qualifications the supplier must present.

The criteria usually encompass 5 different groups: Experience, Quality, Operational, Financial, and Management. Let us review some of the items in each of these areas:

a) Experience

This topic deals with the evaluation of previous experience and past performance regarding the product or service being purchased. The reputation of the supplier in the market and its track record are evaluated under this section.

Visits to the supplier and to other existing customers may show how the supplier has been conducting performance improvements. These improvements may be part of product technology, manufacturing, or business processes.

It is also important to understand how the supplier has honored its contracts, and if the expectations of the other customers are being fulfilled.

b) Quality

Quality is one of the top concerns of any company. A low quality product may destroy the reputation of the company and cost more than a simple loss in sales. Therefore, this topic usually receives a high weight during the evaluation of the suppliers.

Here we analyze the relative level of sophistication of the quality system utilized by the supplier, including the fulfillment of regulatory requirements or mandated quality system registration (e.g. ISO 9000, ISO 14000).

The Sourcing Team should evaluate the quality of the merchandise, the inspection methods used, and the quality levels associated with these inspections. The returns policy may also be part of these analyses.

The most common performance indicators are the percentage of rejections and the number of perfect orders (no errors in volumes, products characteristics, billing, delivery, etc.). These indicators show issues with the part being acquired and with the overall purchasing process.

c) Operational

The criteria evaluated under the 'Operational' segment talks about the supplier's capacity of meeting and sustaining the expectations of the customers.

Capacity does not refer only to men-hours, and machines available to produce at the quality level required, but also the technical ability and capacity to work in cross functional teams with the customers developing new products.

Often, suppliers working in long-term relationships with their customers may have to adapt their processes. Therefore, the willingness to change should be somehow captured. One possible indicator is the number and nature of the improvements made by the vendor. Some examples of these improvements are: the use of innovative delivery methods, e-commerce, on-line systems, MRP, Advanced Planning, and other technologies.

The evaluation may also include a site visit to analyze whether the supplier presents facilities capable of fulfilling their commitments. In addition, according to the type of relationship pursued, the Sourcing Team may evaluate any Research & Development installations.

Remember that the demand may change overnight, but the process and technology necessary to attend to any additional demand may require significant investment and time. Therefore, the evaluation of the operational capability should consider the long-term development of the partners.

The most common performance indicators for the Operation Area are: percentage of on-time deliveries, back order rate, standing orders, and average lead-time.

d) Financial

Of course, no one wants to work with a supplier who is filing for bankruptcy. Therefore, this is a very important section of the supplier's evaluation.

It is essential to establish the financial health of the supplier. An analysis of their financial documents is usually required in order to start this process (e.g. Balance Sheets, Cash Flow, and Income Statements). Another additional piece of information is the credit rating of the organization.

The analysis of their financial documents may also indicate their potential for growth, which may be necessary in a long-term relationship.

Next, the Sourcing Team may analyze the supplier's cost structure in order to identify the potential for improvements and synergies, which may beneficiate both companies.

Finally, the total cost of the transaction should also be analyzed. Remember that we are not discussing only the price of the product, but also the Total Cost of Ownership. Items that should be taken into consideration include: order placement, inspection, quality (e.g. rejects, storage, return and documentation of rejects), environmental (e.g. fees), maintenance, delivery, and inventory requirements.

From a contractual point of view, the total cost may also be affected by payment conditions (e.g. payment terms, discounts), warranties, insurance, and liability coverage. Therefore, these are other items that should be discussed in this section.

e) Management

Under Management, we evaluate the corporate policies, philosophies, and other items that may impact the relationship and were not captured in the previous sections.

Maybe one of the most important items in this section is the cultural match. Many companies like Johnson & Johnson and Marathon Oil require their suppliers to be aligned with their cultural beliefs.

For more than 60 years Johnson & Johnson's values are presented under its "Credo," a one page document translated into 36 languages guiding the actions of their companies across the globe.

Marathon presents its "Code of Business Conduct," where they require their partners to protect Marathon property and information, provide equal opportunity without discrimination, and protect Marathon's reputation among others things.

Other items evaluated in this segment are the vision and ability of the company to manage the business considering long term goals. This should be clear in the supplier business strategy and reflected in other characteristics of the company, such as a continuous improvement philosophy, willingness to share and adopt best practices, and a drive to be a low-cost producer.

The communication with the supplier will also be important. The supplier should present their process for quick responses in case of emergencies or special requests of the customer. The supplier should be committed to customer services and satisfaction.

Keep in mind that before the supplier is chosen, it is highly advisable to run a risk assessment. This analysis should identify possible issues with the suppliers and establish a contingency plan in case of failure. In addition, the Sourcing Team may work on options to mitigate the risk by eliminating or reducing the possible modes of failure.

Chapter 9

Delivery

"Action is the foundational key to all success."

Pablo Picasso

Last year, my good friend Jack started living together with his girlfriend. He was telling me how many changes have happened in his life since she moved in.

"I thought my apartment was big, but now it feels so small. In the shower, I had only a soap bar and a bottle of shampoo. Now I can barely see the soap behind the eleven new bottles she put there. The TV remote is never where it should be. Also, there is the way she folds my clothes, and don't get me started on the way she loads the dishwashers ..."

The start of a new business partnership may be similar to starting a new personal relationship where cooperation is required. At the beginning there will be many adjustments, but if both parts are committed and share the same goals, everything will eventually fall into place.

The Delivery Phase in Strategic Sourcing concerns the adaptation required by the companies to implement the new processes. This is the moment in which the integration between Sourcing and Procurement takes place.

9.1 – Operational Integration

The first step of the Delivery is the Operational Integration. In other words, the Sourcing Team should coordinate the implementation of all changes and adaptations required by the new strategy in order to work with the new partners.

The Operational Integration is a project of its own. The Sourcing Team should define how the changes will be implemented and prepare an adequate implementation schedule.

The Operational Integration may be split in several phases (phased implementation), or it can be done in a single step (big-bang approach). A phased implementation may introduce gradual changes allowing the company time to adapt and cope with the new systems and processes. However, a longer transition time usually means more time until the organization is able to realize the full potential of the strategy being implemented.

The big-bang approach allows for a faster transition, but it is associated with a higher risk due to the higher number of changes introduced simultaneously and the massive quantity of resources required for that.

In addition to the changes for immediate integration, the Sourcing Team should also be concerned with structures for the integration in the long run. The changes will take place in three main areas: Organizational Structure, Resources, and Business Processes.

a) Organizational Structure

When my friend Jack started living with his girlfriend, he noticed some other changes in his life. For example, every other weekend he had to go with his girlfriend to visit his in-laws. Also, since his parents and his in-laws were meeting at his house, he was the one carving the turkey during Thanksgiving.

Basically, this relationship brought Jack into a new hierarchy, and conferred new roles, and responsibilities. These are the same kinds of changes that may be observed during the Operational Integration.

Different strategies may impact the business structure in distinct ways, as well as the functions and responsibilities of different areas. For instance, representatives of the purchasing department may be based in factories, distribution centers, regional offices, or they can be centralized in the

96 📖 *Chapter 9 - Delivery*

headquarters. In addition, they may have different levels of responsibility and authorization according to the strategy defined for each Sourcing Group.

Some processes, such as New Product Development, may require the creation of cross-functional teams. Since these teams may include suppliers, the organizational structure may transcend the boundaries of the company.

New positions and areas may be created or changed to attend the new strategy. For example, those occupying traditional positions, such as Buyer may evolve into Contract Managers or Catalogue Managers, with distinct functions and responsibilities. In other cases, a merge strategy may result into the creation of a cross functional team to execute the merge.

In summary, the Organizational Structure will cover changes related to the hierarchical structure of the company, roles, and responsibilities.

b) Resources

In the first few days under the same roof, Jack realized the house needed some improvements; after all, the place was not "Jack's house" anymore. Now he was in a committed relationship, and, as such, he wanted to make his partner feel ownership for the place. He wanted to create a home for both.

Most of the time, implementing new strategies and establishing new partnerships will require additional resources. Those can be physical assets, systems, people, or others.

Physical assets are all the material resources, such as trucks, scales, containers, and any other equipment necessary for the daily operation.

The new relationship may also require a new set of IT tools to be implemented, or changes in the existing ones. Just to name a few, we may have new ERP Systems, e-business platforms, RFID tags, handheld devices, and Supplier Relationship Management applications (SRM). Therefore, we need to identify and implement the technologies required to support the new strategies.

Additional people may also be necessary in order to implement the new strategy. Consequently, the company may need to hire new employees or identify in their internal pool of resources qualified candidates able to absorb the additional work. The Sourcing Team should also identify the need for training the resources impacted by the implementation.

Other resources that should be considered involve less usual approaches, such as financial instruments, to minimize the risk of a particular strategy (e.g. hedges, swaps).

c) Business Processes

Another point observed by Jack was the new tasks that his relationship brought. Since they were living together, Jack and his girlfriend stop going out so often to bars and restaurants. They started cooking at home more often. Therefore, Jack shared with his girlfriend the responsibility of cooking, setting the table, and loading the dishwasher.

In Strategic Sourcing, that is not different. The alignment of the business processes and information flows are essential to enable new partnerships. The Sourcing Team should establish effective mechanisms to execute and control all the new processes and activities.

For example, purchase requests, purchase orders, spending analyses, non-compliance procedures, and corrective actions are just a few of the many processes that may be impacted by new partnerships.

A new strategy may also involve transferring some internal processes to the suppliers as an outsourcing agreement. Therefore, there are many possible changes in processes that should be considered during the execution of any strategy.

d) Long-Term Integration

Choosing a partner that fits the company's requirements does not mean the relationship will work. Just like any other form of relationship, having a commercial partner implies hard work to maintain the partnership.

Have in mind that the redesign of the Organizational Structure, Resources, and Business Processes should not just enable the relationship with the partner, but also focus on the long-term goals.

Therefore, these structures should at least include tools to manage improvements, track performance, and establish good communication channels.

Every relationship has potential to improve if both parties are committed. In a Strategic Sourcing Organization, people should understand that by helping their partners, they are helping themselves. Consequently, it is important for all the partners to ask at every opportunity what could be done to improve the relationship.

Companies should assume a proactive attitude and look for improvements beyond the boundaries of the organization. Helping a third party to achieve operational improvements may not be an easy task. However, a company can propose improvement programs to motivate the partners to develop in areas such as technology, quality, and product development.

These programs may start with technical evaluations and meetings between specialists of both companies in order to share best practices and establish targets.

In addition, a company may host seminars and promote councils and forums with other suppliers to encourage knowledge sharing and integration.

Performance management will ensure that the company is committed to improving, and that all the goals proposed by the sourcing strategy are being achieved. In order to do that, there should be clear indicators to measure the performance of the internal processes and suppliers.

These key indicators and the appropriate targets may be defined in contracts associated with penalties or bonuses for performance. The indicators will usually capture price, delivery, quality, and service elements.

Whenever a problem is identified, the Sourcing Team should analyze its root cause and take the necessary corrective measures. Every problem brings a disguised opportunity for learning and improving.

Consequently, the company should keep track of all the proposed savings and cost avoidances, monitoring the contract compliances, transaction volumes, and return on investment (ROI) among other things.

Another top priority in all relationships is communication. It is important to always maintain a 2-way communication channel with partners, allowing them to get any clarification, share thoughts, and make suggestions. At the same time, an open communication channel will allow the suppliers to receive feedback and adjust their products and processes to improve the relationship.

Besides the use of councils, forums, and IT tools to improve communication (e.g. SRM, ERP, e-business), the Sourcing Team may also utilize some traditional techniques to be sure that the communication channels are constantly opened.

For example, a "voice of the supplier" survey may be used to benchmark how you perform versus your competition from the point of view of your supplier. This may indicate potential problems and points of improvement in the customer-supplier relationship.

9.2 – Hand-off

The Hand-off is the moment when the Sourcing Team steps back and lets each area start their regular daily operation with the new processes and structures in place.

Depending on the nature of the changes, the Hand-off may involve a short period of assisted operation, where the Sourcing Team will follow closely the areas impacted by the changes in their daily operation.

After the Operational Integration is completed and the strategy is implemented, the Sourcing Team should conduct a final implementation review. This review should be done at the end of the implementation of each Sourcing Group.

During the review, the Sourcing Team will identify and solve any open issues. In addition, the final review is a time when the main findings of the project are summarized in order to be used as a reference in future projects.

The goal is to analyze the entire project, from the steps taken during the creation and selection of the alternatives up to the integration and preliminary results of the respective Sourcing Group. This knowledge should be shared not only with the stakeholders, but also with all the other Sourcing Teams.

During the final review, the Sourcing Team should evaluate the dynamics of the work and level of interaction with the other groups in the company. It is important to be sure that the feedback and suggestions from all the different areas of the company were considered in order to improve future implementations.

9.3 – Follow up

After the strategy for a Sourcing Group is implemented and the final evaluation conducted, the only activity left for the Sourcing Team is the periodical review of the strategy, tracking the savings and evaluating the overall results.

There are no rules for the periodicity of the follow-ups. However, the period in between follow-ups should be at least enough for the new strategy to become stable and new results to be reported. In other words, the strategy should be fully implemented with no outstanding issues, and the time should allow the creation of enough data to discern a trend. For example, the time between follow-ups should be enough to give the business chance to experience the effects of any seasonality.

The first step in this process is to measure the performance of the strategy. That means the use of surveys, formal and informal conversations, data collection (e.g. expenditures, production costs), market analyses, process results, and other means of measurement.

All the collected data should be analyzed and compared to the expected performance as described in the initial strategy evaluation. Note that the

Sourcing Team should be able to isolate the performance of the strategy from any other factors influencing the results.

The results of the analyses should allow the team to understand any trends and possible improvements. In addition, the Sourcing Team should look for compliance with the original plan, and implement any corrective action.

The follow-up cycle ends with the Sourcing Team sharing the lessons learned and results with other areas, teams, and stakeholders. Figure 9-1 shows the basic Follow-up process.

Although the Follow-up is a periodical exercise, remember that the performance of the strategy is continuously monitored through the KPIs defined during the Integration Phase.

In addition, the Strategic Sourcing Area has also the mission of continually monitoring the market to increase the business intelligence for the specific Sourcing Group (e.g. technologies, trends, competitors, etc.)

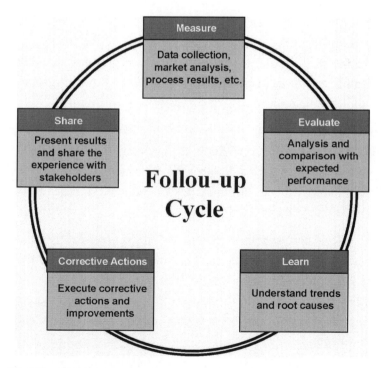

Figure 9-1: Follow-up Process

Chapter 10

Change Management

"It is not enough to conquer; one must learn to seduce."

Voltaire

	6 - Change Management				
1 - Business Case	2 - Profiling	3 - Alternative Creation	4 - Alternative Selection		5 - Delivery

Years ago I was invited to join a communication training session prepared by a psychologist. Unlike other training in this field, which usually teaches the attendants simple communication techniques, that training explored psychological techniques in order to maximize the acceptance of any kind of idea.

One of the most interesting components was a role-playing exercise. The instructor took the role of someone with a personal problem (e.g. alcoholism, depression, relationships) while the rest of the group played friends trying to help him.

However, in order to help the person with the problem the participants could only ask questions. In addition, the questions could not allude to any solution or sound like advice. In other words, instead of asking "Have you tried this solution?" the group should ask "What have you tried?" or "What else do you think you can do?"

This exercise is harder than it sounds. It takes a great deal of practice to master the art of asking the correct question in the correct way. By asking and not suggesting, it is possible to lead the client to the best solution without being in an adversarial position. This technique makes people feel ownership for the idea, and, consequently, makes them more comfortable with the changes.

Chapter 10 – Change Management 103

Asking questions is the first step to help people to start a process of change. By asking questions, we are helping people to confront their paradigms and look into new possibilities.

Not being familiar with a particular subject allows one to create a solution that specialists in the area would not imagine possible. Asking questions in the correct way allows those specialists to re-consider their pre-conceived ideas and accept new alternatives.

Change Management deals with organizational change and works through a number of vehicles, such as communication plans, trainings, stakeholder management, integration exercises, incentives, rewards, benefits, job design, and others.

Change Management is of great importance in initiatives requiring major transformations in philosophies, values, and behaviors. In Strategic Sourcing, the goal is to create a learning organization to constantly improve the intellectual capital of the company. Consequently, Change Management activities will be present in every step of the implementation.

Most of the techniques and tools utilized in Change Management will have a psychological component in order to facilitate the assimilation of the knowledge or adoption of the new behavior.

One common technique applied to many tools in Change Management is the AIPAR model. It stands for the different stages in the change process. They are Awareness, Interest, Preparation, Adoption, and Reinforcement.

Whenever possible, the Change Management professional applies the AIPAR structure in training, communications, or other tools.

In the Awareness Stage, the person or group understands the current situation and the potential effect of their behavior on other people, areas, or processes.

In the Interest Stage, the Change Management professional will introduce the main reasons why the change is necessary. The goal in this stage is to encourage the desire for change.

In the Preparation Stage, the group receives the knowledge and skills necessary to change. In this phase, the willingness to change starts being realized by real actions.

In the Adoption Stage, the changes become part of the daily actions of the group. In other words, this is where the group completes the implementation of the new behavior.

The last stage, Reinforcement, is used to sustain the change through time and to ensure that the message will not fade away.

At the beginning of the chapter, we talked about the exercise where questions were asked in a way that they would not suggest a course of action. This exercise was based on the Constructionist Principle developed by Chris Argyris, a Harvard Business School scholar in the area of Learning Organizations.

He proposed mapping the set of beliefs people have built up over time. Consequently, it would be possible to adapt and present the information about changes in such a way that people with different belief systems could assimilate the new ideas more easily.

Just like in our initial "questions exercise," this principle tries to avoid conflict and facilitate the assimilation of new ideas. Sometimes, the harder we push a change, the harder the group pushes back.

Later, Argyris' work was further developed and presented by Peter Senge in the best seller *The Fifth Discipline*, a well-recognized resource of tools for implementing learning systems.

Briefly, the five disciplines proposed by Senge are:

- Building Shared Vision – The vision of where the group wants to be in the future should be discussed and clearly communicated to everyone.

- Mental Models – This discipline deals with the individual assumptions and generalizations in our own minds. By exploring these models, it is possible to understand the effects they have on our own behavior, and, consequently, to make it easier to understand and adapt to any situation.

- Team Learning – Learning as a group may be harder than as an individual. This discipline encourages an open dialogue and requires the team members to put their own assumptions aside in order to start a group thinking activity.

- Personal Mastery – This discipline is about self-improvement. It deals with the development of skills, such as patience and objectivity. The Personal Mastery discipline encourages us to focus our energies and clarify our thoughts.

- Systems Thinking – This is the Fifth Discipline that integrates the other four. Basically, it promotes the adoption of a holistic view. Each individual learns to look at the whole rather than the parts. Systems Thinking is based on the dynamics of the environment. It allows us to see interrelationships rather than linear cause-effect chains, and processes of change rather than snapshots.

As mentioned before, these Change Management techniques are used by different tools and initiatives such as training, negotiations, presentations, and communications. According to the goals and current work conditions, the Change Management professional will define the best way to facilitate the adoption of a new idea or behavior.

Now that we have a basic understanding of the philosophy behind Change Management, it is possible to describe some of its main goals in the different phases of the Strategic Sourcing implementation.

I - Business Case

In the Business Case, those responsible for Change Management will focus on the stakeholders. The goal is to identify them, understand their interests and motivation, and foresee possible conflicts with the changes Strategic Sourcing brings.

Managing the stakeholders and their expectations is one of the main concerns of Change Management. Those responsible for this area will help the Sourcing Team to introduce all the new concepts, get the buy-in of the stakeholders, and pro-actively access their status.

During the Business Case phase, those responsible for Change Management will ensure the establishment of a two-way communication channel with the stakeholders.

II - Profiling

After the Business Case is approved by the stakeholders, the Project Manager will form the team who will be working on the Strategic Sourcing implementation.

In this phase, Change Management will focus on the selection, training, and development of the project team. Those responsible for Change Management will also help in the definition of communication tools, performance management, reward & recognition systems, and other elements.

In addition, a communication plan should be put in place to announce to the entire company the goals of the project. The Strategic Sourcing philosophy should be reinforced each step of the way in order to minimize the resistance of the organization.

Most of the communication plans involve the following tools: periodical articles on the company's intranet and/or a website answering the most frequently asked questions, promotional material (e.g. shirts, banners), "open-house" events with open forums to clarify any questions, informative presentations, and e-mails from the executive committee highlighting the importance of the project.

III – Alternative Creation

During the Alternative Creation, many new ideas, concepts, and strategies will be discussed. Change Management should help the team to maintain an open mind for possible alternatives. They should be able to explore even unconventional solutions in order to add value to the Supply Chain.

In addition, those responsible for Change Management should promote integration within the team, with the different stakeholders, and areas of the organization.

Despite all the communication, many of the stakeholders will realize the magnitude of the changes only after the Sourcing Team starts presenting the alternatives. Therefore, the Change Management professional should work close to the stakeholders and reinforce the idea that major changes may be necessary to achieve major gains.

IV – Alternative Selection

The focus of Change Management during the Alternative Selection phase is to analyze the potential issues the stakeholder would have with the different alternatives and work on a solution.

At the end of this phase, those responsible for Change Management should be confident that all the stakeholders are comfortable with the selected strategy.

V - Delivery

During the Delivery phase, all the different areas of the company should start their daily operation with the new systems and strategies. Despite the communication plan, a great level of resistance may still be found in the organization at this point.

The focus of Change Management here is to facilitate the assimilation of the new knowledge. Once more, those responsible for Change Management will use the most appropriate tools to achieve this goal. For example, while developing the training plan, different alternatives may be selected, such as on-the-job training, case analyses, lectures, simulations, and others.

Section III
Case Studies

Chapter 11

Mini-case I: Freight Analysis

"The best way to predict the future is to invent it."

Alan Key

During this mini-case, we will focus on the Alternative Creation phase for freight expenses at Rowser Cement, a leader in the cement industry.

Rowser Cement is one of the leaders in the US market, supplying its customers through a broad network of factories and distribution centers spread all over the country.

Cement is a relatively inexpensive product. Its total production cost is usually less than $100 per ton. From a supply-chain point of view, we say that cement has a low value density (cost per volume).

The transport of items with this characteristic usually has a great impact on the margin of the product, since the distribution cost can make it twice as expensive for a particular region. Consequently, freight is a very important component in the cement business.

Since there are sufficient vendors in the transportation business willing to deal with cement, and this kind of service does not require any unusual skill, it is safe to assume that we are talking about a service with "low complexity."

Thus, Freight will fall in the first quadrant of the Strategic Sourcing Matrix (See Figure 11-1), which indicates that Rationalization, Partnerships, and Negotiation strategies are most likely to be used.

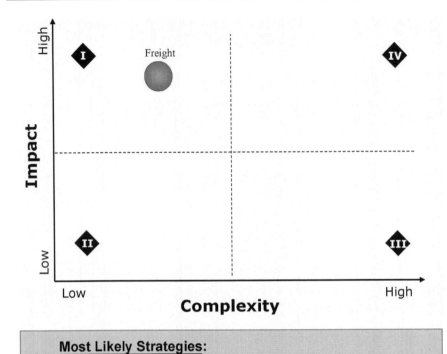

Figure 11-1: Strategic Sourcing Matrix showing Freight for Rowser Cement

11.1 – Rationalization

A typical distribution cost analysis has three main components: Volume, Freight Rates, and Distribution Pattern. The Rationalization exercise will focus on each of these components in order to find opportunities to reduce the consumption of the service.

a) Volume

The volume of freight purchased is directed related to the amount of trucks, barges, and rail cars utilized. This volume may change due to different reasons. The main drivers for the change in volume are:

- Sales Volume – The more the company sells, the more it has to ship to the customers. This is also known as true volume.

- Direct Shipments – In order to reach a specific customer or market, the products may be temporarily stored in a warehouse or distribution center. Although this kind of movement may be necessary to make an operation feasible, it is detrimental to the profitability of the business, and should be minimized. The exceptions to this rule happen when the shipment to a warehouse allows for consolidation of loads and savings in the transportation cost.

- Payload – Payload refers to the utilization of the equipment. In other words, if we can ship a truck with 22 tons of product and we are loading it with only 18 tons, we are underutilizing our assets. In some cases, the product mix will affect the payload, since different products may require special accommodations for each type of vehicle.

- Customer Pick-up – Variations in the volume shipped may also happen due to increases or decreases in the volume picked up directly by customers in the factories or distribution centers.

Most of the customers in the cement business do not plan their purchases ahead of time. They just show up in the distribution centers and buy a truckload. Consequently, an increase in the percentage of direct shipments may be something hard to achieve.

On the other hand, the Sourcing Team identified opportunities to improve the loading process of trucks and railcars. By applying a gentle vibration to the vehicles during the load process, the cement would accommodate better and allow a little extra room for additional volume. Consequently, the new loading process would allow the company to improve their payload.

b) Distribution Pattern

As mentioned before, cement is a product strongly impacted by its distribution cost. Therefore, cement manufacturers carefully choose the location of new plants in order to minimize the transportation cost.

An optimized network of factories and distribution centers allows the cement companies to minimize the distance they have to move their products. Therefore, one of the proposals of the Sourcing Team was to study the network structure and analyze possibilities of improvement by building new distribution centers and selling some of the existing ones.

Another factor that contributes for the reduction on the average shipping distance is accuracy in the production mix plan. The factories should produce the right type of cement as close to the respective consumption market as possible. Consequently, the Sourcing Team's proposal for this item was an improvement in the marketing and production forecasting process.

c) Freight Rates

There are many variables to be considered in the freight rates calculation. It will depend on the transportation modes, negotiation with the carriers, fuel prices, possibility of backhauls, seasonality, accessorial charges, and many other items.

Although freight rates may represent a great source of savings, most of them do not relate to Rationalization. Therefore, savings in this category are usually addressed under Negotiation Analysis.

11.2 – Strategy

After analyzing the business and the transportation market, the Sourcing Team concluded that Vertical Integration was not an option for this company. The variety of transportation modes and the geographic dispersion of the business were counting against any form of vertical integration.

Furthermore, the transportation market for cementitious products was not considered deficient in terms of capacity. Therefore, there was no competitive advantage in such integration.

Consequently, the next step was to analyze possible partnerships in order to improve any of the cost drivers - Volume, Distribution Pattern, and Freight Rates.

The volume of cement produced by the company was already too much for any single carrier to handle. Therefore, there was no point in looking for partners to follow a demand consolidation strategy. On the other hand, there could be some opportunities to consolidate the volume assigned to minor local suppliers and take advantage of national agreements with major carriers.

By analyzing other companies with products and business structures with similar characteristics, the Sourcing Team concluded that a partnership with some competitors could be a good alternative to pursue.

For instance, let us take as an example one of Rowser Cement's main plants in the south of California. This is one of the closest factories to their distribution center in Texas. Therefore, they have regular shipments between these locations paying $70/ton of cement.

At the same time, one of its main competitors produces the same type of cement in a plant in New Mexico and ships it to their distribution center in the San Francisco area, paying $65/ton. These movements are illustrated on the map in Figure 11-2.

By joining forces, each company could supply each other's distribution centers and save on distribution costs. The haul from South California to North California would cost $24/ton and from New Mexico to Texas $32/ton. Assuming an initial agreement to supply 4,000 tons/year, they could realize combined savings of $316,000/year.

The Sourcing Team identified 25 other lanes as potential candidates for a similar agreement with this and other competitors. The savings opportunities were estimated at over $5 million/year.

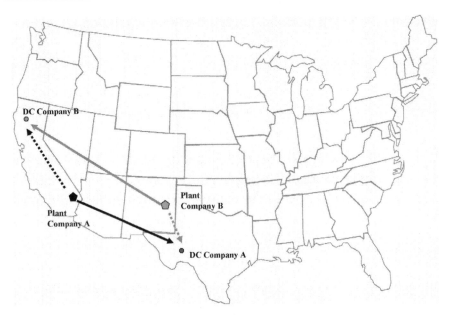

Figure 11-2: Example of Swap Strategy for Rowser Cement

In fact, this kind of "swap strategy" is not new in the market. Shell in South Africa has similar exchange agreements with other oil companies. Even other leaders in the cement business, such as Lafarge and Cemex utilize similar agreements.

Of course, it is easier to talk than to actually implement these kinds of supply agreements. Besides creating an elaborated optimization model to define the best swap options, it might still be necessary to convince the senior executive of both companies into working with their competitors. It means that we may have to change a mentality that may have been going on for years already, and is thus engraved in the minds of the most traditional executives.

11.3 – Negotiation

Since the volume of total business in the US is more than a single carrier can handle, Rowser Cement has leverage in the negotiation. On top of that, there are other things the company should take into consideration that may affect the average freight rate.

The first concern is with the variation in the rates throughout the year. Cement is a seasonal product with a higher demand in warm months. Therefore, carriers may charge a premium for having to work at full capacity during peak months.

The recommendation of the Sourcing Team was for Rowser Cement to avoid spot rates as much as possible by improving their production and sales planning and getting into rate agreements early in the year in order to achieve lower rates in exchange of a committed volume.

In addition, the Sourcing Team proposed the analysis of the trade-off between Inventory and Distribution. By operating in off-peak season, it would be possible to take advantage of lower transportation rates. On the other hand, the inventory costs and capacity in their distribution centers and warehouses would have to be carefully analyzed.

The improvement in the planning, and the capacity to communicate the requirements to the carriers in advance would also allow for a better mix in transportation modes, which could drive the average freight cost down.

Finally, since the fuel cost was one of the main factors responsible for the variation in the freight rate along the year, the Sourcing Team proposed the use of financial instruments in order to create a hedge against the variation of the oil price in the international market.

11.4 – Organizational Structure

Improvements in Organizational Structure may help to reduce the costs related to the purchase and utilization of logistics services.

One of the conclusions of the Sourcing Team was that the organization would work best with a centralized negotiation for global and national contracts, but there was the need of a local logistics representative in each region or in specific factories, warehouses, and distribution centers in order to assure quality and satisfactory reaction time for any unexpected event. Besides the coordination and control of the services, the local logistics representative could make agreements with local carriers that could react quicker to last minute requests. The volume of the local contracts would be limited.

Another activity centralized in the headquarters would be logistics planning. This plan would be aligned with the marketing and production areas going through periodic reviews during the Sales and Operations Planning meetings.

One last organizational recommendation was a better alignment with the international trading office of the company. This office would be responsible for negotiating the best alternatives to import cement.

Although there was an extra cost associated with the importing operation, the incremental demand could improve the distribution pattern by creating a new sourcing point in the network (port of entry of the imports), and cover any production shortage.

11.5 – Conclusion

The Sourcing Team summarized all the alternatives in a simple table presented on Table 11-1.

At the end of the Alternative Creation phase, the team also performed a SWOT Analysis for each option showing the main strengths (e.g. strategic fit, potential savings), weaknesses (e.g. difficulty to implement), opportunities (e.g. development of the suppliers in order to improve quality, capacity, and cost), and threats (e.g. economic and political risks).

The analyses for the different alternatives were presented in detail to the Steering Committee for their final approval before allowing the team to proceed to the Alternative Selection phase.

Sourcing Group	Component	Drivers	Alternatives	Responsible Area
Freight Cost	Volume	- Sales Volume - Direct Shipment - Payload - Customer pick-up	• Motivate customers to order from factories • Improve equipment utilization	Sales/ Marketing Logistics
	Distribution Pattern	- Average Distance	• Increase accuracy in Sales Forecast • Increase accuracy in Production Plan • Optimize Distribution - centralized • Review Network of facilities • Partnership with competitors • Imports	Sales/ Marketing Operations Logistics Supply Chain Supply Chain/ Logistics Supply Chain/ Purchasing
	Rates	- Base Rate - Accessorials - Fuel Surcharge	• Consolidation of Vendors • Review business requirements • Re-negotiate contracts (centralize negotiations) • Benchmark rates • Timely negotiations • Contracts with lowest rates (avoid peak season) • Hedge	Logistics/ Purchasing Logistics Logistics/ Purchasing Logistics/ Purchasing Logistics/ Purchasing Logistics/ Purchasing Logistics/ Finance

Table 11-1: Summary of Alternatives for Freight at Rowser Cement

Chapter 12

Mini-case II: Capital Investment

"Leave no stone unturned to help your clients realize maximum profits from their investment."

Arthur C. Nielsen

This mini-case focuses on the Alternative Selection among different Capital Investment strategies. During this exercise, it will be possible to see the need for correctly identifying the different costs and options for a purchasing strategy. In addition, this mini-case shows the importance of the alignment between the sourcing strategy and the overall business strategy.

This case analyzes a juice producer in Europe. This organization is part of a Chinese beverage company trying to expand its business presence in Europe.

As mentioned in Chapter 6, Capital Expenditures is one of the four major categories of products that can be purchased by a company. The assets in this category range from items of small value, such as furniture and computer accessories, to expensive items, such as the construction of a whole new plant.

The main goals of Strategic Sourcing in capital purchases are:

- to ensure that the expenditure is aligned with the overall strategy of the company;

- to analyze different options in order to choose the best alternative to fulfill the objectives of the purchase;

- to help with identifying the best suppliers; and

- to create the most efficient purchasing process based on the assets acquired.

After a comprehensive study, the European branch of a Chinese juice producer concluded that they could expand their customer base in Europe by investing in a new marketing campaign. Nevertheless, their factories in the region were already operating at full capacity.

After consulting the engineers, factory managers, logistics team, and trading specialists, the Sourcing Team had three options on their hands.

The first option was the expansion of one of the factories and implementation of a new production line.

The second option was the upgrade of all the lines in an existing plant in order to improve their speed, resulting in a gain in capacity slightly superior to the first option.

Finally, the third alternative would require some investment in an existing marine terminal in order to receive imports from Asia. However, the only factory in Asia that could supply this product had limited available capacity that was less than the expected incremental market demand.

In order to compare the different options, the Sourcing Team collected detailed information associated with each option. The data included information on the total cost incurred in each scenario throughout the life of the project.

Prior to the calculation of the financial impact, the Sourcing Team shared the assumptions with all the stakeholders and got their agreement that those statements were an accurate representation of the reality of the company. A list summarizing the main assumptions for each scenario is presented on Table 12-1.

After the validation of the assumptions, the Sourcing Team built simplified Cash Flows utilizing a standard template adopted by the company. This template assumed a total of 20 years (8 explicit and 12 implicit). At the end of that period, no salvage value was considered for the assets. In addition, the model did not assume inflation, continuing value, or price increases. The Cash Flows for the different options are presented on Tables 12-2, 12-3, and 12-4.

122 📖 *Chapter 12 –Mini-case II: Capital Investment*

	General Info	OPTION 1: New Production Line	OPTION 2: Factory Upgrade	OPTION 3: Imports
VOLUME	Incremental Demand: First Year - 6 MM units Second Year - 9 MM units Third Year and forward - 12 MM units	Sourcing Capacity: First Year - 8 MM units Second Year - 12 MM units Third Year and forward: 12 MM units	Sourcing Capacity: First Year - 10 MM units Second Year - 14 MM units Third Year and forward - 14 MM units	Sourcing Capacity: First Year - 4 MM units Second Year - 6 MM units Third Year and forward - 8 MM units
INVESTMENT	Cost of Capital: 10% Financials for 20 years (8 explicit) No residual/ salvage value	Investment € 35 MM	Investment € 40 MM	Investment : € 5 MM
MARKETING	€ 2.3 MM for 100% of the volume € 2 MM for 70% or less of the volume	Marketing: € 2.3 MM	Marketing: € 2.3 MM	Marketing: € 2 MM
COGS	Standard cost: 0.9/unit	COGS: 0.8/unit Lower energy consumption Less raw material waste Additional direct labor required	COGS: 0.7/unit No additional direct labor required	COGS: 1.8/unit Import duties High delivery cost
OVERHEAD	Admin/ Production Overhead	Additional personnel Increase in maintenance Increase in costs in other facilities	No additional personnel required Increase in maintenance	No additional Prod./Admin. Overheads No maintenance required

Table 12-1: Summary of assumptions for Alternative Selection

OPTION 1: New Production Line

Year	0	1	2	3	4	5	6	7	8	9 to 20
Units Sold		6,000	9,000	12,000	12,000	12,000	12,000	12,000	12,000	12,000
Net Sales		*€ 18,000*	*€ 27,000*	*€ 36,000*	*€ 36,000*	*€ 36,000*	*€ 36,000*	*€ 36,000*	*€ 36,000*	
Variable Distribution		(1,200)	(1,800)	(2,400)	(2,400)	(2,400)	(2,400)	(2,400)	(2,400)	
COGS		(4,800)	(7,200)	(9,600)	(9,600)	(9,600)	(9,600)	(9,600)	(9,600)	
Other Variable		(360)	(540)	(720)	(720)	(720)	(720)	(720)	(720)	
Total Variable Costs		**(€ 6,360)**	**(€ 9,540)**	**(€ 12,720)**	**(€ 12,720)**	**(€ 12,720)**	**(€ 12,720)**	**(€ 12,720)**	**(€ 12,720)**	
Production Overhead		(1,000)	(1,000)	(1,000)	(1,000)	(1,000)	(1,000)	(1,000)	(1,000)	
Admin Overhead		(200)	(200)	(200)	(200)	(200)	(200)	(200)	(200)	
Fixed Distribution		(1,200)	(1,200)	(1,200)	(1,200)	(1,200)	(1,200)	(1,200)	(1,200)	
Marketing		(2,300)	(2,300)	(2,300)	(2,300)	(2,300)	(2,300)	(2,300)	(2,300)	
Other Fixed		(400)	(400)	(400)	(400)	(400)	(400)	(400)	(400)	
Total Fixed Cost		**(€ 5,100)**	**(€ 5,100)**	**(€ 5,100)**	**(€ 5,100)**	**(€ 5,100)**	**(€ 5,100)**	**(€ 5,100)**	**(€ 5,100)**	
Depreciation		(2,333)	(2,333)	(2,333)	(2,333)	(2,333)	(2,333)	(2,333)	(2,333)	
Gain/Loss - Equip. Sale		-	-	-	-	-	-	-	-	
Pre-Tax Income		*€ 4,207*	*€ 10,027*	*€ 15,847*	*€ 15,847*	*€ 15,847*	*€ 15,847*	*€ 15,847*	*€ 15,847*	
Tax Expense		(1,683)	(4,011)	(6,339)	(6,339)	(6,339)	(6,339)	(6,339)	(6,339)	
Net Income		*€ 2,524*	*€ 6,016*	*€ 9,508*	*€ 9,508*	*€ 9,508*	*€ 9,508*	*€ 9,508*	*€ 9,508*	
Add Back Depreciation		2,333	2,333	2,333	2,333	2,333	2,333	2,333	2,333	
Investment	(35,000)			-	-	-	-	-	-	
Net Cash Flow	**(€ 35,000)**	**€ 4,857**	**€ 8,349**	**€ 11,841**	**€ 11,841**	**€ 11,841**	**€ 11,841**	**€ 11,841**	**€ 11,841**	**€ 88,752**

*Values in € '000s

Table 12-2: Cash Flows of the New Product Line Alternative

124 📖 *Chapter 12 –Mini-case II: Capital Investment*

OPTION 2: Factory Upgrade

Year	0	1	2	3	4	5	6	7	8	9 to 20
Units Sold		6,000	9,000	12,000	12,000	12,000	12,000	12,000	12,000	
Net Sales		*€18,000*	*€27,000*	*€36,000*	*€36,000*	*€36,000*	*€36,000*	*€36,000*	*€36,000*	
Variable Distribution		(1,200)	(1,800)	(2,400)	(2,400)	(2,400)	(2,400)	(2,400)	(2,400)	
COGS		(4,200)	(6,300)	(8,400)	(8,400)	(8,400)	(8,400)	(8,400)	(8,400)	
Other Variable		(360)	(540)	(720)	(720)	(720)	(720)	(720)	(720)	
Total Variable Costs		(€5,760)	(€8,640)	(€11,520)	(€11,520)	(€11,520)	(€11,520)	(€11,520)	(€11,520)	
Production Overhead		(500)	(500)	(500)	(500)	(500)	(500)	(500)	(500)	
Admin Overhead		(100)	(100)	(100)	(100)	(100)	(100)	(100)	(100)	
Fixed Distribution		(1,200)	(1,200)	(1,200)	(1,200)	(1,200)	(1,200)	(1,200)	(1,200)	
Marketing		(2,300)	(2,300)	(2,300)	(2,300)	(2,300)	(2,300)	(2,300)	(2,300)	
Other Fixed		(400)	(400)	(400)	(400)	(400)	(400)	(400)	(400)	
Total Fixed Costs		(€4,500)	(€4,500)	(€4,500)	(€4,500)	(€4,500)	(€4,500)	(€4,500)	(€4,500)	
Depreciation		(2,800)	(2,800)	(2,800)	(2,800)	(2,800)	(2,800)	(2,800)	(2,800)	
Gain/Loss Equipment Sale		-	-	-	-	-	-	-	-	
Pre-tax Income		*€4,940*	*€11,060*	*€17,180*	*€17,180*	*€17,180*	*€17,180*	*€17,180*	*€17,180*	
Tax Expense		(1,976)	(4,424)	(6,872)	(6,872)	(6,872)	(6,872)	(6,872)	(6,872)	
Net Income		*€2,964*	*€6,636*	*€10,308*	*€10,308*	*€10,308*	*€10,308*	*€10,308*	*€10,308*	
Add Back Depreciation		2,800	2,800	2,800	2,800	2,800	2,800	2,800	2,800	
Investment	(42,000)	-	-	-	-	-	-	-	-	
Net Cash Flow Liquido	**(€42,000)**	**€5,764**	**€9,436**	**€13,108**	**€13,108**	**€13,108**	**€13,108**	**€13,108**	**€13,108**	**€98,245**

* Values in € '000s

Table 12-3: Cash Flows of the Upgrade Alternative

OPTION 3: Imports

Year	0	1	2	3	4	5	6	7	8	9 to 20
Units Sold		4,000	6,000	8,000	8,000	8,000	8,000	8,000	8,000	8,000
Net Sales		*€ 12,000*	*€ 18,000*	*€ 24,000*	*€ 24,000*	*€ 24,000*	*€ 24,000*	*€ 24,000*	*€ 24,000*	
Variable Distribution		(800)	(1,200)	(1,600)	(1,600)	(1,600)	(1,600)	(1,600)	(1,600)	
COGS		(7,200)	(10,800)	(14,400)	(14,400)	(14,400)	(14,400)	(14,400)	(14,400)	
Other Variable		(240)	(360)	(480)	(480)	(480)	(480)	(480)	(480)	
Total Variable Costs		**(€ 8,240)**	**(€ 12,360)**	**(€ 16,480)**	**(€ 16,480)**	**(€ 16,480)**	**(€ 16,480)**	**(€ 16,480)**	**(€ 16,480)**	
Production Overhead		-	-	-	-	-	-	-	-	
Admin Overhead		-	-	-	-	-	-	-	-	
Fixed Distribution		(800)	(800)	(800)	(800)	(800)	(800)	(800)	(800)	
Marketing		(2,000)	(2,000)	(2,000)	(2,000)	(2,000)	(2,000)	(2,000)	(2,000)	
Other Fixed		(400)	(400)	(400)	(400)	(400)	(400)	(400)	(400)	
Total Fixed Costs		**(€ 3,200)**	**(€ 3,200)**	**(€ 3,200)**	**(€ 3,200)**	**(€ 3,200)**	**(€ 3,200)**	**(€ 3,200)**	**(€ 3,200)**	
Depreciation		(333)	(333)	(333)	(333)	(333)	(333)	(333)	(333)	
Gain/Loss - Equipment Sale		-	-	-	-	-	-	-	-	
Pre-tax Income		*€ 227*	*€ 2,107*	*€ 3,987*	*€ 3,987*	*€ 3,987*	*€ 3,987*	*€ 3,987*	*€ 3,987*	
Tax Expense		(91)	(843)	(1,595)	(1,595)	(1,595)	(1,595)	(1,595)	(1,595)	
Net Income		*€ 136*	*€ 1,264*	*€ 2,392*	*€ 2,392*	*€ 2,392*	*€ 2,392*	*€ 2,392*	*€ 2,392*	
Add Back Depreciation		333	333	333	333	333	333	333	333	
Investment	(5,000)	-	-	-	-	-	-	-	-	
Net Cash Flow	**(€ 5,000)**	**€ 469**	**€ 1,597**	**€ 2,725**	**€ 2,725**	**€ 2,725**	**€ 2,725**	**€ 2,725**	**€ 2,725**	**€ 20,427**

* Value in € '000s

Table 12-4: Cash Flows of the Imports Alternative

In the Cash Flows we can observe the difference in COGS, Marketing, Net Sales, and Maintenance (overhead). Based on that, it was possible to calculate the three financial indicators used by the company in order to compare the different alternatives (Internal Rate of Return - IRR, Payback, and Net Present Values – NPV). These indicators are presented in Table 12-5.

	OPTIONS		
	1 - New Line	2 - Upgrade	3 - Imports
IRR	30.4%	28.6%	40.9%
NPV - 10% cc*	€ 56,577	€ 59,885	€ 15,219
Payback	3.2	5.0	3.9

* Values in € '000s

Table 12-5: Financial Indicators of the Alternatives

While the first option (New Line) presents the quickest payback, the second alternative (Factory Upgrade) has the best Net Present Value, and the third (Imports) the highest IRR.

Besides the financial indicators, the Sourcing Team still had to consider an additional decision criterion: the strategic fit. The final proposal should be aligned to the overall strategy of the company.

Considering that the European market was looking for expansion, the second alternative (Factory Upgrade) would better fit their strategy since it would give the company the production capacity required by the new marketing campaign and still create a little extra available capacity for future growth. However, this alternative was also the one with the worst return and payback. Therefore, the European executives would have to evaluate their willingness to sacrifice their profitability in exchange of the additional market share.

On the other hand, the headquarters in China had other investment proposals from its other companies around the world competing with the proposals from the European market.

Since the resources for investment were limited, China was focusing on investments with high profitability. Therefore, the headquarters established a minimum of 35% IRR for all investments. Under these circumstances, Option 3 (Imports) seemed the most adequate alternative.

In the end, the dilemma caused by the strategies conflict (local and global) was presented to the Steering Committee, which decided to negotiate with China for an exemption from the minimum IRR rule.

Although Option 2 (Factory Upgrade) would give extra capacity for future improvements, this option would require higher capital and was presenting lower returns. Therefore, the Steering Committee decided to present to China with Option 1 (New Line) as the preferred alternative.

As demonstrated in this mini-case, although financial indicators are important to compare different options, they should not be seen as the only criteria. Strategic Sourcing always encourages a holistic approach to the analyses, and the focus on the long-term plans of the organization.

Chapter 13

Mini-case III: Raw Material

"The best thing about the future is that it comes only one day at a time."

Abraham Lincoln

This mini-case focuses on the Alternative Creation for the raw materials in Bongo Watches. For years, this company has been responsible for one of the favorite digital quartz watches brands in a small country in South America.

One of Bongo Watches' strengths is the constant reinvigorating of its portfolio of products by introducing new models every few months. However, due to the growing number of newcomers in the market, Bongo Watches decided to start a Strategic Sourcing implementation to become more competitive.

A few months into the implementation, the Sourcing Team reached a point where they started analyzing the Raw Materials. Basically, their watches were composed of a circuit board, microchip, quartz crystal, display, battery, case, wrist strap, and pins to set the time.

During the Profiling Phase, these materials were grouped into 5 Sourcing Groups: Microelectronics (circuit boards, microchips, and crystal), Displays, Batteries, Case (Case and Pins), and Strap.

By analyzing simultaneously the different groups considered raw materials, the Sourcing Team expected to have a better understanding of the entire finished product, since any change in the concept of the product could affect all the raw materials.

The Strategic Sourcing Matrix in Figure 13-1 places the Strap and Case as low complexity items since their production method is relatively simple, and there are plenty of suppliers in the market. On the other hand, the Microelectronics, Batteries, and Displays have a slightly more complex production method. Therefore, they were considered to be of high complexity. All the groups were considered to be of high impact, since they were raw materials purchased in great quantity by the company.

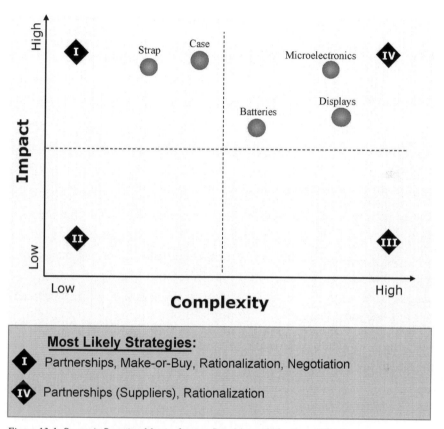

Figure 13-1: Strategic Sourcing Matrix showing Raw Materials for Bongo Watches

13.1 – Rationalization

Rationalization of raw materials implies the reduction of the waste during the manufacturing and assembling processes, or the reduction of the consumption of the materials by restructuring the product being created.

130 📖 *Chapter 13 –Mini-case III: Raw Material*

Bongo Watches operated under an assembly-to-stock model. All the different components were bought from reliable suppliers, and the final product was assembled in-house.

Analyzing the data collected throughout the project, the Sourcing Team concluded that the waste of raw material during the assembling process was already low, and any changes would not have any significant impact on the business. Therefore, the focus during the Rationalization was the possible redesign of the product.

In fact, since the company's strategy was based on constantly launching new products, the Rationalization should not cover only the existing products, but also implement a systematic approach to assure the best usage of the raw material for all new products.

The Sourcing Team decided to use a simplified Value Engineering Analysis (VEA). VEA, also known as Value Engineering or Value Analysis, is a technique developed by General Electric during the Second World War. Due to the shortage of resources during that time, the company started using this technique in order to find possible substitutes for their raw materials.

The idea is to identify the main functions performed by the product and allocate to them the cost of the raw materials used. This will determine the cost of each function and allow a fair comparison against the value perceived by the market.

Bongo Watches carries 80 different models, targeting 2 different markets – high-end customers and athletes. The VEA was performed for the top 10 products, responsible for 90% of the sales of the company.

In the first step of the VEA, the Sourcing Group worked with marketing representatives in order to identify the main functions performed by the product. As a result, the team came up with dozens of different functions. The main ones were grouped as follows:

A – To show time

B – To show date

C – To be precise

D – To allow easy visualization of the information.

E – To be resistant (e.g. shock-proof)

F – To be humidity proof

G – To be water proof

H – To show social status

I – To feel comfortable

J – To have endurance (e.g. battery)

Next, the group discussed with the engineers the best way to allocate the cost of the materials to each function. For example, the team had to define what the incremental cost of avoiding humidity was, and which parts in the watch were responsible for that function.

Once the functions were identified and their costs established, the marketing team conducted different analyses involving the target market in order to determine the perception of the customer. In other words, how much they were willing to pay to have that specific function present in the watch.

A VEA Summary Table analyzing one of the main products and comparing it with the perception of the high-end customers is presented in Table 13-1.

Have in mind that VEA is not a simple cost cutting exercise. It should be seen more like cost tuning, where the results will allow the designers, marketing group, and engineers to create more economical alternatives to accomplish the function, respecting the original characteristics of the product.

As we can see in Table 13-1, Bongo Watches was investing $0.55 to include Function D in their product. In other words, they were expending this amount to let the customers easily visualize the information on the watches.

132 📖 *Chapter 13 –Mini-case III: Raw Material*

Bongo Watches Model: 1025	COMPONENTS								Function Total Cost	Cost %	Market Perception Function Total Cost	Market Perception Cost %
	Circuit Board	Microchip	Crystal	Display	Battery	Case	Pins	Strap				
A - To show time	0.06	0.05	0.02		0.02				0.15	3%	0.40	9%
B - To show date	0.06	0.05	0.02		0.02				0.15	3%	0.40	9%
C - To be precise	0.01	0.02	0.02		0.01				0.06	1%	0.30	7%
D - To allow easy visualisation of the info				0.55					0.55	13%	0.40	9%
E - To be resistant (e.g. shock)				0.05		0.35	0.02	0.03	0.45	10%	0.45	10%
F - To be humidity proof						0.10	0.02	0.05	0.17	4%	0.35	8%
G - To be water proof						0.30	0.02	0.30	0.62	14%	0.10	2%
H - To show social status						0.50	0.02	0.30	0.82	19%	0.85	19%
I - To be comfortable						0.45	0.01	0.40	0.86	20%	0.80	18%
J - To have endurance (e.g. battery)					0.50				0.50	12%	0.40	9%
Component Cost:	0.13	0.12	0.06	0.60	0.55	1.70	0.09	1.08	4.33	100%	4.45	100%
Component % of Total Cost:	3%	3%	1%	14%	13%	39%	2%	25%	100%			

* *High-end customers*

Table 13-1: VEA Summary Table Analyzing Bongo Watches and high-end customers' perception

However, the market believes this function value was only $0.40. Therefore, the company was overspending in order to have this characteristic in the product.

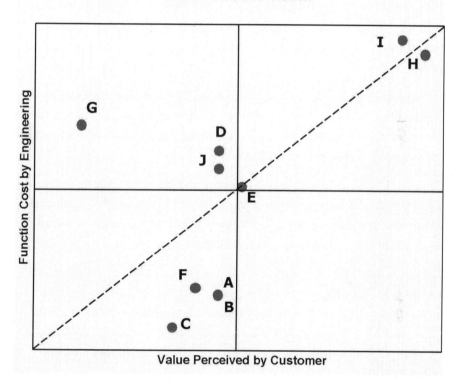

Figure 13-2: Value vs. Cost Matrix for high-end customers at Bongo Watches

The results on the table allowed the Sourcing Team to draw similar conclusions for 3 other functions – water proofing, comfort, and endurance.

The chart in Figure 13-2 shows another way to visualize the main opportunities comparing the engineering cost and the value perceived by the customer.

All the attributes falling above the diagonal line have a relative cost higher than the value perceived by the customer. Therefore, it is necessary to study the specifications for the components contributing to the higher than expected cost of these functions in order to create more economical alternatives.

In order to correct the Engineering Value of the overpriced functions, the Sourcing Team worked with designers, engineers, and representatives from the main suppliers, and came up with a list of possible actions for each function.

The ease of visualization of the information (Function D) could have its cost reduced by a slight reduction of the LCD display, and making better use of its remaining area. They concluded that the numbers could be easier to read, even with a smaller display.

Based on the low value gave by the market for the water proof function (Function G), new research was requested from the Marketing Specialist, which confirmed that this was not a function the target customer would require. Therefore, it was eliminated from the product.

For comfort (Function I), the Engineering Team worked with one of the suppliers in order to create a thinner case with the same resistance and design of the original. The back of the case was made of stainless steel, but the remainder of the case was a lightweight titanium alloy. In addition, the finishing of the leather strap was improved to provide a more pleasant sensation.

Finally, in order to affect the endurance of the product (Function J), the engineers studied the life span of the battery. At the end, the team changed it to a more affordable and less powerful version lasting only 4 years instead of 6 from the initial concept.

All these changes allowed the product to maintain the main characteristics required by the target market for less than the expected cost.

Since future plans include the introduction of models with advanced technologies, the company also prepared a VEA for the new athletic watch with radio-transmitter. The VEA Summary Table is shown in Table 13-2.

Chapter 13 – Mini-case III: Raw Material 📖 135

Bongo Watches
Model: 3056

FUNCTION	Circuit Board	Microchip	Crystal	Display	Battery	Case	Pins	Strap	Function Total Cost	Cost %	Market Perception Function Total Cost	Market Perception Cost %
A - To show time	0.06	0.05	0.02		0.02				0.15	3%	0.30	5%
B - To show date	0.06	0.05	0.02		0.02				0.15	3%	0.30	5%
C - To be precise	0.01	0.02	0.02		0.01				0.06	1%	0.25	5%
D - To allow easy visualisation of the information				0.60					0.60	11%	0.60	11%
E - To be resistant (e.g. shock)				0.20		0.40	0.02	0.03	0.65	11%	0.70	13%
F - To be humidity proof						0.10	0.02	0.05	0.17	3%	0.40	7%
G - To be water proof						0.30	0.02	0.30	0.62	11%	0.65	12%
H - To show social status						0.50	0.02	0.30	0.82	14%	0.05	1%
I - To feel comfortable						0.45	0.01	0.40	0.86	15%	0.40	7%
J - To have endurance (e.g. battery)					0.50				0.50	9%	0.60	11%
K - Radio-transmission	0.35	0.35			0.25	0.15			1.10	19%	1.30	23%
Component Cost:	**0.48**	**0.47**	**0.06**	**0.80**	**0.80**	**1.90**	**0.09**	**1.08**	**5.68**	**100%**	**5.55**	**100%**
Component % of Total Cost:	**8%**	**8%**	**1%**	**14%**	**14%**	**33%**	**2%**	**19%**	**100%**			

* Athletic customers

Table 13-2: VEA Summary Table Analyzing new watch model and Athletic Customers' perception

136 📖 *Chapter 13 –Mini-case III: Raw Material*

Once more, through the Value vs. Cost Matrix in Figure 13-3, it is possible to visualize the Functions the group had to focus on while analyzing the new athletic model.

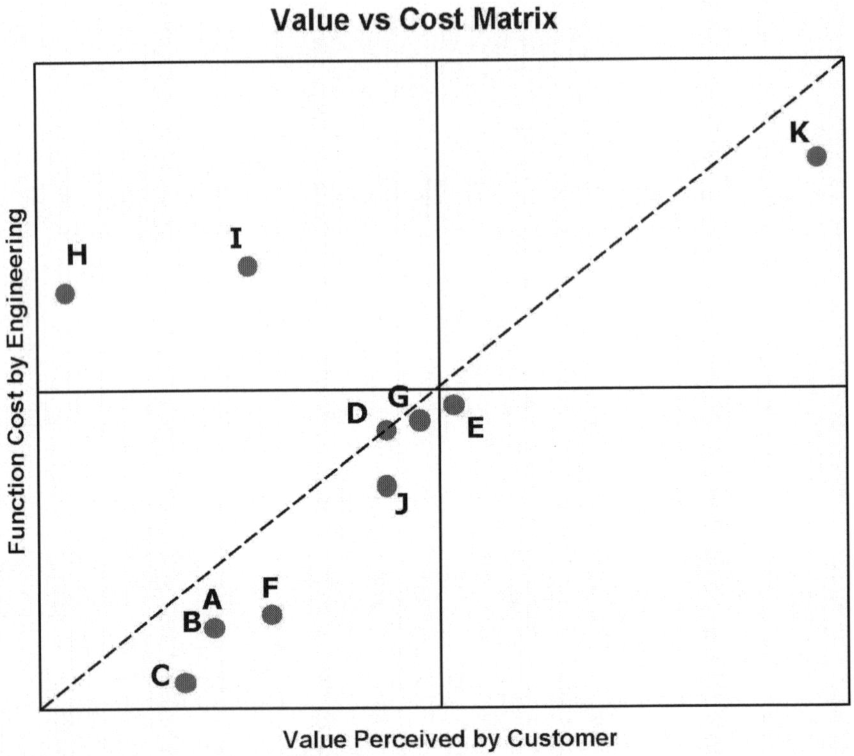

Value vs Cost Matrix

Figure 13-3: Value vs. Cost Matrix for the new product and athletic customers at Bongo Watches

Marketing specialists, designers, engineers, and suppliers worked together to analyze possible solutions for reducing the cost of the comfort, and social status functions.

After some research, the group of specialists concluded that the cost targets could be reached by substituting the material used in the strap by a flexible and resistant synthetic rubber. This would still give the product the same athletic look, with additional comfort. In addition, following the same concept discussed for the high-end customer model, the case would be made of a new lightweight titanium alloy.

The Social Status Function would have its cost decreased by eliminating the stamp with the name of the brand placed on the strap, and the logo carved on the back of the case. The only branding information would be placed on the display of the watch.

In summary, this simplified VEA was the tool chosen by Bongo Watches to help them to conduct a rationalization study during the development of new project concepts.

More than a simple mathematical exercise, the simplified VEA was the communication tool used during the interaction of all the different departments involved in the development of new products. This tool would assure Strategic Sourcing that any new product was going through a rationalization study for the raw materials utilized.

13.2 – Strategy

The business strategy followed by Bongo Watches was clear: they position themselves as an innovative company, constantly introducing new models in the market.

From the Rationalization point-of-view, the Sourcing Team was able to introduce a tool aligned to the overall strategy of the company. During the Strategy analysis, the challenge was to find partners to live up to the expectations of this fast-paced product development environment.

Due to the nature of the business, the Sourcing Team was not able to identify any new partnership opportunities associated with Competitors, Substitutes, Customers, or New Entrants.

Furthermore, since the company had already researched potential suppliers, Bongo Watches counted with a large portfolio of national and international vendors for the raw materials.

Finally, trying to be aligned with the company's overall strategy, the Sourcing Team proposed the reduction of the number of suppliers in order to reach a better integration during the development of new products.

13.3 – Negotiation

The supplier consolidation proposed during the strategy analysis would improve Bongo's leverage during the negotiations.

Another change in the relationship with vendors was the introduction of long-term contracts. This kind of initiative allowed the suppliers to make bigger commitments by opening offices in the country were Bongo Watches maintained its headquarters.

In addition, the new relationship established bonuses for productivity, quality, and improvements brought by their vendors. The idea was to maintain a healthy relationship where both sides could be rewarded for their commitment.

13.4 – Organizational Structure

Organizational Structure was one of the areas most affected by all the proposed changes. The closer interaction with the suppliers for the development of new products required a complete redesign of the organization.

Purchasing the right thing at the right price would not work if they were not able to make it to the market on time. Therefore, the focus of the Sourcing Team was to streamline not only the purchasing process, but also the entire product development process.

The first change was the adoption of a web-based platform where different suppliers could contribute on-line for the new projects. For example, based on marketing inputs, the microchip and circuit suppliers could propose different options that would be further analyzed by the other suppliers in order to define their contributions to the project.

This e-platform would have several forms of web interaction (e.g. chat rooms, instant messenger), and all the relevant information about the participants of the project. This initiative would allow new products to get to the market 50% faster, and with less quality issues.

Moreover, some suppliers decided to place a representative into Bongo's facilities in order to improve the services by tracking inventory, helping with product development, addressing quality issues, and working on demand planning.

The implementation of these changes was a great challenge in terms of Change Management, since they would not affect only Bongo Watches, but also the suppliers.

13.5 – Conclusion

Taking the marketing strategy into consideration is important in all phases of the project, including during the Alternative Creation as demonstrated in this mini-case.

In Bongo Watches' example, it was also possible to see how different groups are impacted by Strategic Sourcing. In order to establish a common communication and analysis approach across different organizations, a company can use many different tools. The simplified VEA and the web-based platform for new product development were examples of these tools.

Companies in fast-pace environments should work on their communication and be flexible while searching for alternatives. Communication is always an important factor in any form of relationship and should never be neglected in Strategic Sourcing projects.

Chapter 14

Frequently asked questions

"You know that children are growing up when they start asking questions that have answers."

John J. Plomp

For the second edition of this book, I included this bonus chapter with some of the most common questions in Strategic Sourcing. These questions were collected in presentations, discussions with other professionals, and in some of the most popular forums on the Internet.

I hope the comments below help companies and professionals to understand the trends of this powerful concept and how it is evolving in the current world.

1 – How Strategic Sourcing companies react to the market crash?

In a very simplistic view, we can say that the main cause for the recent market crash was the collapse of credit in the mortgage industry. Soon, everyone was concerned about credit, the market lost its liquidity, and the population reduced its level of consumption in several categories.

The lack of credit meant that less cash was available and it was more expensive to access it. Therefore, the volume of transactions in the market plunged. Inventory levels went up, and prices became more volatile.

The general problem was the poor visibility into the future because end-customer purchase forecasts were harder to get, and suppliers were intimidated by the credit crunch and afraid of a potential supply disruptions from reduced operations.

Suddenly, many companies had more suppliers then they could utilize and very little liquidity (credit) to buy anything.

The best strategy in this kind of scenario is to take the opportunity to re-evaluate the needs of the company and the relationship with the suppliers. Some of the recommended steps are:

a) Reevaluation of Suppliers:

- Intensify supplier audits.
- Tighten supplier-rating programs.
- Evaluate current credit policies with suppliers.
- Improve focus on risk assessment (supplier capacity and financial health).
- Consider opening new-supplier development programs.

b) Revision of Purchasing Budgets:

- Reevaluate material needs based on volumes and existing inventories.
- According to the forecast of prices, inflation, and demand, define a new purchasing budget according to the material/service group to be purchased.

c) Benchmarking & Internal Study

- The slowdown of the economy allows time to understand the business and seek new opportunities.

d) Adjust Target of Existing Partnerships

- Delay purchases and seek less expensive options
- Re-evaluate supply agreements.

e) Cash Management Projects

- Conserve capital.
- Initiate new cost reduction efforts.

142 📖 *Chapter 14 –Frequently asked questions*

> ## 2 - Which is more important: Financial Analysis or Non-Financial Evaluation?

It is a mistake to think Financial and Non-Financial evaluations are unrelated. At the end of the day, all the evaluations have the same goal: to ensure that the company will maximize its results.

Therefore, this should not be an either/or question. Both criteria, financial and non-financial, should be used to assess a strategy or specific supplier. The non-financial evaluation will allow us to determine whether the financial results proposed by a possible partnership can really be achieved.

It is very common to see companies taking short-cuts while performing non-financial evaluations of partnerships. The evaluator trusts his gut feeling for important key factors, such as the assessment of their corporate culture, or how proactive, reliable, or creative the supplier is.

Because they are often subjective, non-financial evaluations can introduce a higher risk to the equation. Nevertheless, they can also show that the numbers on the financial evaluation may not make sense.

Remember that numbers alone never tell the entire story. The more you know about a partner, the more you reduce the risk of failure in a relationship.

> ## 3 - Is there any way to predict whether a partnership will be successful?

Successful partnerships usually depend on two factors: synergies and ability to work together.

By synergies, we mean the addition of two factors where the final effect is greater than the sum of their individual achievements. For example, companies may seek partners with technologies, products, or structures that complement their own. The more opportunities for synergies partners have, the higher are the chances of a successful partnership.

The ability to work together is the other fundamental piece in the partnership equation. Just like in a personal relationship, it may be very challenging to work with a partner with different values and expectations. The best partnerships are formed by organizations that have a clear vision of their role and realistic expectations of the results. In addition, they share common values and have the same level of commitment and respect for each other.

One suggestion for organizations seeking successful partnerships is to make things as simple and transparent as possible. Simplify the processes, clarify the expectations (e.g. financial and non-financial goals, responsibilities, etc), share the vision, and plan for the future (e.g. new products, new ideas, new technologies that may be included in the scope of the partnership).

4 - How important is alignment in executing your business strategy?

It is important to remember that when we talk about alignment we should not only think about the alignment with our suppliers, but also the alignment within our own company. Everyone in the organization should share the same values and objectives.

Poor alignment with suppliers may lead to issues with processes, products, and even influence the opinion of your clients regarding your company. If suppliers and clients do not share the same vision for a common process, we may have a miscommunication that can cause delays, rework of orders, and many other issues that will add cost and put at risk our capacity of delivering the finished products to your clients.

Remember that problems in the alignment of suppliers may happen due to different expectations, strategies, cultures, processes, and levels of commitment among many other factors.

The best way to ensure clients and suppliers are aligned, is to perform a detailed evaluation of the partnership and make the expectations clear before starting working together. After that, the best strategy is to establish an honest and open dialogue, and stimulate a continuous discussion about performance and growth of the partnership.

Wal-Mart, for example, has announced that Sustainability is a key pillar of their strategy and set long-term environmental goals in order to capture the estimated 16% of the US population who was classified as LOHAS consumers (Lifestyle of Health and Sustainability). This is a $209 billion market.

Wal-Mart goals include utilizing 100% renewable energy, creating zero waste, and selling products that sustain our resources and environment.

In order to have their suppliers aligned to these new objectives, Wal-Mart developed a scorecard to evaluate their partners where the environmental impact of packaging and production is taken into consideration.

The "eco-friendly" trend has grown tremendously in the mind of the end customers in the last few years. Therefore, many retailers like Wal-Mart are focusing on this opportunity and changing their entire supply chain, expecting the alignment of their partners.

This phenomenon should not come as a surprise for CEOs. Business alignment has always been present in many different supply chains. From quality certifications to cost reduction programs, companies have always been trying to get aligned to the expectation of their partners.

---

5 – What is Supplier Relationship Management?

Supplier Relationship Management (SRM), or Supplier Performance Management (SPM), is a collection of practices to enhance the strategic relationship between the buyers and suppliers. It streamlines and makes more effective the processes between a company and its suppliers.

There are many concepts behind effective SRM, but the main ones commonly applied are: *Accountability, Development, Integration, Value Creation,* and *Performance Management.* These are outlined below:

Accountability is concerned with the existence of clear structures and processes to allow the partners to understand who is responsible for each activity they share. It is advised that companies have one main contact in each side that will defend their respective interests. In order to do that, this person will maintain frequent dialogues with his counterpart, analyze and work on any open issue, and be sure all the responsible parts are performing as expected.

Development is based on the idea that the supplier is now part of your company. Consequently, the company should consider developing the supplier, providing training, exploring new opportunities, developing new products, etc. It is important to have in mind that this is not a one-way street. In other words, suppliers should also consider training their strategic clients and involve them in any developing activity.

Integration is another key concept for SRM. Operational processes (e.g. order placement and delivery) should be coordinated in order not to cause any disruption of the Supply Chain. The same applies for planning information (e.g. forecast, sales projection, inventory levels), which should be shared between strategic partners to achieve higher efficiency and lower costs.

Values Creation is about setting goals and performance targets. Some of the common targets include total savings, material price reductions, lead-time, quality rate, and perfect orders. However, value creation is not measured only by hard benefits. Soft benefits, such as access to new technologies, are also considered as goals of the relationship.

Performance Management is another fundamental concept in SRM. By tracking the performance of the suppliers, it is possible to identify improvement opportunities, top performers, top offenders, and take the appropriate actions. These actions can go from adjusting the targets up to the disqualification of the supplier, and consequently, the breakup of the partnership.

146 📖 *Chapter 14 –Frequently asked questions*

---

6 – Does Strategic Sourcing apply for small business?

Absolutely! There are great examples of small businesses that are taking advantage of Strategic Sourcing. Some of them may not go through the formal process of creating a Sourcing Tree or building a Strategic Sourcing Matrix, but they usually work hard to identify the source of their main expenses and creative ways to remain competitive.

In this book, we talked about Kitcharm, a small company in South America that used strategic sourcing concepts since its creation in order to survive in the market. They identified the key components of their supply chain and decided to adopt a vertical integration strategy.

Some other small companies do exactly the opposite. Some great examples can be observed in a few restaurants in Manhattan. In order to reduce their costs, they outsourced their non-core activities, such as taking reservations.

When you call these restaurants to make a reservation, you're in fact talking to a call center in India, China, or in any other part of the world, where they do the same service for several other restaurants. Due to the demand consolidation, they can do this service cheaper than if the restaurants hired someone specifically for that purpose. In addition, they are available 24h/day, 7 days/week to take your reservation.

Small companies usually purchase a smaller variety of products than big companies do. Therefore, it may be easier for them to focus on and implement any changes. Nevertheless, they may still have to use creative thinking to find the best savings alternatives.

---

7 – What is best: buy or lease?

Buy versus lease is a classic question discussed by executives in most companies. There are many different elements to consider in this kind of analysis. In order to make the best decision, the company should consider their financial goals and strategies (e.g. Cash Flow and P&L impact), ability to finance their projects, relationship with suppliers, and other soft savings.

Sometimes, the financial and non-financial elements make the analysis so complex that different analysts in a company can reach to completely different conclusions. In order to illustrate the complexity of such analysis, let us take the buy versus lease decision for a fleet of trucks:

a) Financial Goals and Strategies

Some companies are driven solely by growth in profits. Some others are willing to sacrifice profits to increase their market share. They believe, once their slice of the market is big enough, they can gradually increase their profit margin. In other words, each company may have different strategies, which will drive their financial goals.

Consequently, the first step for a Lease versus Buy analysis is to clearly understand the financial goals of the company, and measure the impact on the Cash Flow and P&L for each case. Remember that we are talking about a comparison based on the Total Cost of Ownership (e.g. purchase price, maintenance, gas consumption, residual value, etc).

In addition, some organizations may decide to put aside the financial analyses and lease trucks instead of buying them just because they want to focus all their time and energy on the core business of the company, which may be producing something rather than managing a fleet of vehicles.

b) Access to cash

Smaller companies and entrepreneurs usually have limited access to cash. In other words, it is harder for them to finance new projects. Therefore, they may prefer to lease the trucks, and invest any resource they can put their hands on (e.g. bank loans) in projects with a higher return.

In addition, cost of capital for entrepreneurs may be higher than the leasing cost. Therefore, leasing may be a more attractive alternative for smaller companies.

c) Relationship with Suppliers

Another reason for choosing one strategy or another is the relationship with suppliers. It is important to understand who would be providing the trucks, maintenance, financing, and any other service associated with the chosen strategy.

The availability of suppliers in the market, their capacity, reliability, and how easy it is to work with them are key factors in this kind of decision.

d) Other Soft Savings

- Speed of innovation (carbon footprint, capacity, mileage).

- Age of fleet.

Many factors in this kind of analysis are very hard to estimate. For example, leases may have many other intangible advantages over owning a fleet. Short-term leases may keep the fleet with a lower average age, not only reducing many maintenance issues, but also giving to the market the impression of a modern and reliable company that is always re-investing in improvements.

Moreover, the use of leases may allow the company to replace the trucks more often and take advantage of the latest innovations in trucks (e.g. eco-friendly trucks, higher capacity, less fuel consumption).

In summary, "Lease versus Buy" is always a complex decision that should not be analyzed solely on its financial merit. Many other strategic considerations are involved in this kind of analysis, and even similar companies in the same market may reach different conclusions.

> **8 – Is there any pre-work we can do in order to simplify the implementation of a Strategic Sourcing program?**

Strategic Sourcing is a very complex and broad subject. The more you know the market, the company, and its products, the easier the implementation will be.

Chapter 14 –Frequently asked questions 149

There are many healthy habits a company can develop to facilitate the implementation of Strategic Sourcing. One of the most effective observed in many organizations is *Stook-keeping Unit (SKU) Rationalization.*

Several companies analyze periodically (every 2 to 4 years) the number of SKUs in their portfolio. Some of these SKUs present low volume sales in the last few years, are very costly to handle, have a low contribution margin, or are very slow moving items. These items add complexity to the operation and are usually removed from the portfolio of the company.

There are many books and different kinds of software that support SKU Rationalization studies. Just be careful to understand the method they adopt, since some software may suggest a method that does not fit the reality of your company.

For example, some software may consider only the profitability of each SKU without adopting a holistic approach. In other words, we may decide not to discontinue SKUs with low margins and sales if they generate other types of profits throughout their useful lives, such as after sales services, additional components, sales of complementary products, etc.

In addition, there may be a strategic reason behind the existence of a low profit SKU in the product portfolio. For example, the item may be necessary to offer a full range of products to the largest customer. Without that item, the customer could decide to buy from a different supplier.

Finally, you need to observe the trend and study the market prior to deciding to remove any SKU from the company's portfolio. Although some items have been moving very slowly in the last few years, you may observe a trend indicating that the sales of a particular SKU are getting stronger every day.

The rationalization of the number of SKUs usually helps during the construction of the sourcing tree and, consequently, throughout the entire Strategic Sourcing implementation.

Bibliography

Ansoff, Igor. Corporate Strategy. Pan Macmillan, 1986.

Anthes, Gary H. "Case Study: Supply Chain Whirl." Computerworld 9 June 2005. 23 Aug. 2007 <http://www.computerworld.com.au/index.php/id;1550407298;fp;4;fpid;1398720840>.

Argyris, Chris. On Organizational Learning. 2nd ed. Blackwell Limited, 1999.

Banfield, Emiko. Harnessing Value in the Supply Chain: Strategic Sourcing in Action. Wiley, 1999.

Baumann, Hans O. "Value Engineering Analysis (VEA)." Project Management Institute - Switzerland Chapter. 11 Nov. 2003. Nestlé. 23 Aug. 2007 <http://www.pmi-switzerland.ch/autumn03/2-autumn03-vea.pdf>.

Brusick, Philippe, Ana M. Alvarez, Lucian Cernat, and Peter Holmes, eds. Competition, Competitiveness and Development: Lessons From Developing Countries. United Nations Conference on Trade and Development, 2004, United Nations. 23 Aug. 2007 <http://icps.ftc.go.kr/data/master/2005/01/000002/000002_01.pdf>.

"Change Management." Wikipedia. 23 Aug. 2007 <http://en.wikipedia.org/wiki/Change_management>.

Drucker, Peter F. The Practice of Management. Collins, 1993.

Greaver, Maurice F. Strategic Outsourcing: a Structured Approach to Outsourcing Decisions and Initiatives. AMACOM/American Management Association, 1999.

Gray, John. Men Are From Mars, Women Are From Venus. Thorsons Publishers, 1993.

Hamnmer, Michel, and James Champy. <u>Reengineering the Corporation, a Manifesto for Business Revolution</u>. New York: HarperBusiness, 1993.

"Joint Sales and Distribution Agreement of Electronic Materials for 'Wafer Level Packaging'." <u>BASF Group</u>. 14 Feb. 2007. 23 Aug. 2007 <http://sustainability.basf.com/en/presse/mitteilungen/pm.htm?pm id=2571&id=V00-R4levAyvFbcp3-Q>.

Lamb, Robert B. <u>Competitive Strategic Management</u>. Prentice Hall, 1984.

Laseter, Timothy M. <u>Balanced Sourcing: Cooperation and Competition in Supplier Relationships</u>. 1st ed. Jossey-Bass, 1998.

Massin, Jean-Philippe. "How to Plan a Strategic Sourcing Program - SSOA IV/IV." <u>Strategic Sourcing | Europe</u>. 12 Dec. 2006. 23 Aug. 2007 <http://www.massin.nl/eSourcing/2006/12/12/how-to-plan-a-strategic-sourcing-program-ssoa-iviv/>.

Massin, Jean-Philippe. "How to Scope Purchases - SSOA Part I/IV." <u>Strategic Sourcing | Europe</u>. 12 June 2006. 23 Aug. 2007 <http://www.massin.nl/eSourcing/2006/06/12/strategic-sourcing-opportunity-assessment/>.

Massin, Jean-Philippe. "Strategic Sourcing by... A.T. Kearney 2004." <u>Strategic Sourcing | Europe</u>. 3 Nov. 2006. 23 Aug. 2007 <http://www.massin.nl/eSourcing/2006/11/03/strategic-sourcing-by-at-kearney-2004/>.

Miles, Lawrence D. <u>Techniques of Value Analysis and Engineering</u>. 2nd ed. TX: McGraw-Hill, 1972.

Newmann, Dirk, Carsten Holtmann, and Thomas Honekamp, comps. <u>Market Integration and Metamediation: Perspectives for Neutral B2B E-Commerce Hubs</u>. Information Management and Systems, University Karlsruhe. 23 Aug. 2007 <http://www.iw.uni-karlsruhe.de/Publications/NeumannHoltmannHonekamp_MarketI ntegration_S67ff.pdf>.

Ohmae, Kenichi. <u>The Mind of the Strategist: the Art of Japanese Business</u>. 1st ed. McGraw-Hill, 1991.

152 📖 *Bibliography*

Park, Richard. <u>Value Engineering: a Plan for Invention</u>. CRC, 1998.

Rothfeder, Jeffrey. "Some Experts Blame Rising Software Prices on Microsoft." <u>CNN.Com</u>. 11 Jan. 1999. 23 Aug. 2007 <http://www.cnn.com/TECH/computing/9901/11/microrise.idg/>.

Sagar, Nikhil. "CPFR At Whirlpool Corporation: Two Heads and an Exception Engine." <u>IBF</u>. Winter 2003. Institute of Business Forecasting. 23 Aug. 2007 <http://www.ibf.org/Downloads/Winter_03-04_Article.pdf>.

Seecontrol. "ABB Robotic Division Implements Successful Vendor-Managed Inventory Program." <u>KnowldegStorm.Com</u>. 1 Jan. 2007. 23 Aug. 2007 <http://whitepaper.intelligententerprise.com/shared/write/collateral /CST/51803_90196_99718_!QVM6MA02M1LRSCI_ABB_MRO _CaseStudy01-22-2007-02-35-01-PM.pdf?ksi=1458061&ksc=1274920872>.

Senge, Peter M. <u>The Fifth Discipline - the Art and Practice of the Learning Organization</u>. Doubleday Currency, 1990.

"Supplier Qualification." <u>Marathon</u>. 1 Jan. 2007 <http://www.marathon.com/Our_Values/Diversity/Supplier_Diver sity/Supplier_Selection_Criteria/>.

"Suppliers Resources." <u>Johnson & Johnson</u>. 23 Aug. 2007 <http://www.jnj.com/supplier_resources/policies/selection_criteria .htm;jsessionid=IGJDRWVECTN5WCQPCCEGU3AKB2IIWTT 1>.

"Technology Facts & Figures." <u>Women's Learning Partnership</u>. 23 Aug. 2007 <http://www.learningpartnership.org/resources/facts/technology>.

Tichy, Noel M. <u>Managing Strategic Change: Technical, Political, and Cultural Dynamics</u>. Wiley, 1983.

Volgelstein, Fred. "Steve Jobs Owns Your Living Room." <u>Fortune</u> 30 Jan. 2006. 23 Aug. 2007 <http://money.cnn.com/2006/01/27/technology/pluggedin_fortune /index.htm>.

White, Erin. "The Domino's Theory to Keeping Employees." <u>Brand Autopsy</u>. 14 Mar. 2005. The Wall Street Journal. 23 Aug. 2007 <http://brandautopsy.typepad.com/brandautopsy/2005/03/the_dom inos_the.html>.

Womack, James P. <u>The Machine That Changed the World : Based on the Massachusetts Institute of Technology 5-Million-Dollar 5-Year Study on the Future of the Automobile</u>. Scribner, 1990.

Printed in Great Britain by
Amazon.co.uk, Ltd.,
Marston Gate.